D1479231

PRAISE FOR *MENTAL HEALTH WARRIOR*

"I had the privilege of working beside CW4 Cliff Bauman in uniform and witnessed his leadership. His tireless work ethic, optimism, and wisdom were always inspirational to those who were fortunate enough to be in his orbit. If, as they say, 'Adversity is a terrible thing to waste,' Cliff Bauman certainly exemplifies that important warrior mindset. Cliff understands the struggle of post-traumatic stress because he's personally lived in its dark shadow. Cliff is indeed a true 'Mental Health Warrior,' and his life experiences are described in searing detail in Dr. Kammerer's important account."

—**Col. John Fenzel (USA, Ret.), author of** *The Lazarus Covenant*

"Cliff Bauman is a true mental health warrior, patriot, and pioneer. Unlike many in the country, Cliff Bauman has firsthand experience, looking for people at the Pentagon on 9/11. Cliff was traumatized by what he saw, but packed away this trauma, just like he did his uniform and his boots from that day. Years later, these emotions took over as he attempted to end his own life. Cliff Bauman is a modern 'everyman' in our culture today. His triumphant story deserves to be told to everyone in the country, both inside and outside the military. I am proud to call him my friend."

—**Danei Edelen, founder of the National Alliance on Mental Illness (NAMI) Brown County affiliate**

"Dr. Kammerer brings readers through events that transpired at the Pentagon on 9/11 by presenting a gritty recollection of the events, as told by three National Guard first responders and many survivors, including me. Chief Warrant Officer Clifford Bauman, a young soldier at the time, put his heart into his work for three days, and when what he gave was not enough, it almost killed him. Combining Chief Bauman's personal story with the accounts of many other first responders and survivors of the Pentagon on 9/11 and other traumatic events, plus insight from his years as a suicide prevention professional and forensic psychologist, Dr. Kammerer takes the reader through the harrowing event of 9/11, detailing the torment, PTSD, and survivor's guilt that afflicts first responders' psyches. Chief Bauman's story is worthy of the reader's attention, and Dr. Kammerer draws the reader in while taking them out of the story enough to instill valuable lessons about how we think, why we react the way we do, and how to change both. I believe this is a good read for not only soldiers and veterans, but also civilians, as it applies to humans across the board."

—**Dr. Richard E. Talley, Colonel (Ret.), US Army**

"If we truly want to care for those in pain, we must first find the courage to not only share our stories but learn from those brave enough to share theirs. The stories of Clifford Bauman and his battle buddies will no doubt test and grow each reader's resilience and strength. Cliff's story will show you that suicide is by far not a cowardly act, in fact the opposite. Readers will gain yet more understanding and hopefully possess the courage to become their brother's keeper."

—**Nick Cottrill, USA 1SG (Ret.), CEO and co-founder of *Veteran Trash Talk***

MENTAL HEALTH
WARRIOR

A TRUE STORY OF SUICIDE
AND SURVIVAL AFTER 9/11

BASED ON THE STORY OF
CHIEF WARRANT OFFICER 4 CLIFFORD BAUMAN
WRITTEN BY **WILLIAM D. KAMMERER, PH.D.**

an imprint of Amplify Publishing Group

www.amplifypublishing.com

Mental Health Warrior: A True Story of Suicide and Survival After 9/11

For more information, please contact:

Amplify Publishing, an imprint of Amplify Publishing Group
620 Herndon Parkway, Suite 220
Herndon, VA 20170
info@amplifypublishing.com

Library of Congress Control Number: 2022918512

CPSIA Code: PRV0623A

ISBN-13: 978-1-63755-418-0

Printed in the United States

DISCLAIMER

CONTENTS

CHAPTER 1

THESE WERE NOT ACCIDENTS

LOCATED JUST OUTSIDE OF WASHINGTON, DC, in Arlington, Virginia, the Pentagon is the center of US military decision-making and leadership. All senior Department of Defense (DoD) officials work from the Pentagon, including the Secretary of Defense, the Secretaries of the Army, Air Force, and Navy, and the Joint Chiefs of Staff, which include the Chiefs and Vice Chiefs of the Army, Marine Corps, Navy, and Air Force. Additionally, a mountain of other high-level military and civilian DoD officials work at the Pentagon, along with their support staff. At the height of World War II, the Pentagon was the place of employment for about 30,000 defense personnel, including military members, DoD employees, and contractors. It was the place of work for about 20,000 employees on September 11, 2001.

Situated on 29 acres, the Pentagon is possibly the largest office building in the world and is arranged into five rings, with ten corridors running from the outside of the building to a courtyard in the center of the building. The prefix "Penta-" derives from the Greek word for "five," and Pentagon refers to a shape with five angles. This running theme of five shows up throughout the Pentagon's design. There are five sides, five rings dissecting the office building, five stories in height, and a five-acre courtyard in the center of the building, as well. The five concentric rings, labeled A through E, divide the Pentagon into layers, and ten corridors intersect the rings, going from the outside of the building (E-Ring) to the center of the building (A-Ring) where the courtyard sits.

The five-sided design of the building with dissecting corridors is ostensibly an efficient shape because an employee who knows the way can walk from any office or area in the structure to any other in less than ten minutes. However, the building's configuration, with its corridors, wedges, floors, escalators, and stairwells, can make going from one point to another an unnerving task for personnel without extensive knowledge of the space. In all, there are over 17 miles of hallways covered by the ten corridors. Thirty-foot spaces between each set of rings provide light to the offices situated there. An important beltway, called the A-E Drive, runs across the space separating Rings B and C.

The C-Ring is the central ring of the five and is an open ring with stairwells going between all five floors of the Pentagon. The C-Ring is more open than the other rings and allows for vehicles to operate in the building. The Pentagon was constructed in the 1940s, and the concrete was set by hand—likely with the use of plywood and human physical exertion. Biscuit-shaped impressions in the concrete from the plywood are still visible, and there is a joke going around the Pentagon that there were scores of lower-rank enlisted soldiers and sailors holding the forms in place.

The Pentagon was constructed during World War II to make room for the increasing War Department, led by Chief of Staff George C. Marshall and approved by President Franklin D. Roosevelt. Before its construction, the War Department was decentralized across seventeen Washington, DC, buildings. The official groundbreaking for the construction of the Pentagon began on September 11, 1941, and was completed in January 1943 at a cost of more than $80 million. Sixty years to the day after the groundbreaking ceremony, the Pentagon would be remorselessly attacked by a shadowy terrorist organization named al-Qaeda. This story starts with that attack.

Dulles International Airport, in the DC suburbs of Chantilly, Virginia, 27 miles from the Pentagon, is one of three airports serving the DC Metro area. The other two are the Baltimore/Washington International Thurgood Marshall Airport in Baltimore, Maryland, 35 miles from the Pentagon, and the Reagan National Airport in Arlington, Virginia, two miles from the Pentagon. At 8:10 in the morning on September 11, 2001, American Airlines Flight 77 departed for Los Angeles International Airport with 64 people on board. The flight made an abrupt and unexpected U-turn to head back toward the east an hour after takeoff, and communications between the plane and air traffic controllers on the ground were cut off. Three other flights in different locations at the same time also unexpectedly deviated from their paths.[1]

About 90 minutes later, at 9:37 a.m., Arlington County Fire Department and Police Department personnel in different areas noticed a low-flying aircraft heading toward the Pentagon. American Airlines Flight 77 collided into the west side of the Pentagon at a speed exceeding 530 miles per hour. The point of impact was at the E-Ring, between corridors 4 and 5. Similar crashes happened in New York City at 8:46 a.m. and 9:03 a.m. These were not accidents.

CHAPTER 2

THE CELL PHONE WARRIORS

THE PENTAGON BANNED SMOKING IN THE building in the mid-1990s. Smokers had to sneak out to A-E Drive for a smoke. A-E Drive was a very important site during the 9/11 attacks, as personnel were able to escape from the dense black smoke to safety, out the windows of the B and C Rings, between corridors 4 and 5 on the west side of the Pentagon. The lights shining through A-E Drive windows gave personnel inside the tragedy hope and a means of escape.

Back in September 2001, Chief Warrant Officer 2 (CW2) William Clifford Bauman (Cliff) was a telecommunications manager at the National Guard Bureau and was the contracting representative for a cell phone contract with AT&T Wireless, among other telecommunications duties. The way contracts go, vendors change often, and AT&T had recently picked it up after Verizon's contract ended. Senior Airman Robert "Bob" Hewett worked for AT&T, and he and Cliff had gotten to know each other on a professional level.

Bob was 35 at the time, with a flat-top haircut that he still maintains, and he was about six feet tall and 150 pounds. He has always been athletic—running the two-mile physical fitness test in eleven minutes. He has military discipline and a gift for sarcastic comedy and feigned indifference. Bob was an avionics technician for C-130 aircrafts with the Rhode Island Air National Guard, but he worked in Maryland. He was sitting in the Network Operations Center (NOC) for AT&T Wireless in Beltsville, Maryland, about 20 miles from the Pentagon. His team was watching American Airlines Flight 11 hit the World Trade Center North Tower—the news was reporting that it was a small airplane that hit. Senior Airman Hewett was smarter than that.

"Something is not right. That was not a small plane. Can't you see that it is a full-size plane? Something bigger is going on!"

Bob was correct. Seventeen minutes later, United Airlines Flight 175 hit the second of the Twin Towers, the South Tower. He raced back home to Pasadena, Maryland, and grabbed his uniform, loaded all his weapons, and put one near each door. It was obvious to him what was happening. The country was under attack, and he was likely to be called on to defend it.

"Bob, what is this all about?"

"Angelina, a lot of good people just died. If anyone comes through the door, you know what to do."

Having set up a defense for his home and prepared his wife in case the attack moved closer to their house, Bob went back to work at the AT&T Network Operations Center. Thirty-five minutes after the second plane hit the World Trade Center, the attackers turned their sights on the headquarters of the United States Department of Defense.

The tragedy unfolded. The Pentagon was struck.

AT&T lines were busy with all types of queries from people trying to find ways to help, as they do during difficult times. One customer called the sales floor and asked a sales engineer if they had a way to track cell phone signals to find missing people. That question found its way to Bob, working one floor below the sales team. At the time, people were using flip phones that did not have the GPS systems that were incorporated years later. The only way to track cell phones at the time was by looking at the cell sites to see if a specific cell phone registers. That method would only give cell phone site data, which would not include any measures of exact location, such as latitudes or longitudes. Cell phone *site* data can tell first responders what sector the cell phone is in, or which cell phone tower they are in range of.

Wreckage of the Pentagon after the attack. Photo credit: Shutterstock.

There was one other way to help first responders search for survivors with cell phone location, though. Tracking cell phone *signals* would require being on the ground in the sector with electronic gear including a spectrum analyzer and a high-gain, directional "Yagi" antenna. A first responder with these items would see activity on the spectrum analyzer if the cell phone was on, and only when someone was calling their cell phone. It was a long shot, but it had a chance of saving lives. The junior enlisted avionics technician, Senior Airman Bob Hewett, called CW2 Bauman with the idea.

Now the army acts quickly. Soldiers are motivated and perform well under pressure. Soldiers take action. Cliff started moving on Bob's idea immediately.

A third soldier, CW2 Jack Du Teil, was one of Cliff's good friends who worked with him in the Jefferson Plaza 1 building located in Crystal City, about half a mile south of the Pentagon. The building was, in a manner of speaking, across the street from the Pentagon. At twelve stories tall, the sightline from the roof was high enough to see the Pentagon. Jack and his noncommissioned officer in charge were watching the smoke billow out of the Pentagon from the roof of the Jefferson Plaza building, thinking about what they could do, when Bob showed up with his equipment.

Bob was a traditional airman for the Air Force, meaning he worked his civilian job full-time, and just attended military drills about one weekend a month. However, like many national guardsmen, his civilian job was related to his military specialty;

that is how he fit into the picture. He had the technical expertise and the equipment to help. Everyone at the National Guard building was feeling helpless, watching the tragedy and chaos. Our nation had just been attacked on our own soil and on a scale that had not been seen since Japan's attack on Pearl Harbor on December 7, 1941.

Cliff called Jack and explained that he had another guard member who believed he had a plan to help rescue survivors. He needed approval from higher levels of leadership to get into the site. Jack worked for a three-star general and his deputy, a two-star general. As members of the Joint Staff, they were the leaders in charge of the National Guard. The Pentagon was sending someone from the Joint Staff Secretariat section to brief Jack's section. The two-star General Secretariat was in the middle of an emergency update briefing when Jack went into the meeting, stood up, and addressed the room of leaders.

"Sir, one of our warrant officers who oversees a cell phone contract has technology that can be deployed at the scene and may be able to find any survivors that are trapped. I am requesting permission to go to the Pentagon with him and his contractor to see if we can be of help."

"Yes, get out of here. Just give me an After-Action Review tomorrow."

CHAPTER 3

THIS IS MY CRIME SCENE

THE YEAR 2001 WAS STILL THE dawn of personal cell phone ownership, and they were nowhere near as pervasive as now. AT&T was an up-and-coming cell phone company. Its competitors were Verizon, Cingular, Sprint, and T-Mobile. Each company communicated on their own frequency. AT&T operated at the 3G 1900 PCS bands in the 1850–1990-megahertz (MHz) range, so the team used an antenna that could receive signals in that spectrum. Verizon and Cingular worked at a lower range of 850 MHz, and Sprint and T-Mobile were in the 1900 MHz range. The team's antenna would pick up everything but the Verizon or Cingular signals. Longer antennas transmit and receive shorter wavelengths; therefore, receiving Verizon and Cingular transmissions would require a different antenna. Starting at the front sections of the A-Ring, between corridors four and five, the team proceeded into the doorways and windows of the collapsed area of the Pentagon to reduce interference from other signals, scanning the center frequencies of the AT&T, Sprint, and T-Mobile bands with a 100 MHz spread.

Once approved to use their equipment to search for survivors, things rolled quickly.

After a couple of calls and some hasty movements, Senior Airman Hewett and Jared—the AT&T Government Account Manager who initially requested volunteers to assist at the Pentagon—and three other AT&T employees—David, Zach, and Albert—were at Jefferson Plaza 1 with two spectrum analyzers, a "Yagi" directional antenna, and all the required RF connectors and cables and power cords. They picked up Cliff and Jack, the two Chief Warrant Officers, and sped to the Pentagon. The sales engineer, Jared, and the other AT&T employees were not in the military, and they had to stay back, leaving Cliff, Jack, and Bob to perform the search. The other AT&T employees were called away to assist with increasing the call capacity around the Pentagon. Jared stayed and supported them technically and logistically throughout the day.

The team arrived at the Pentagon at about 1:30 p.m., and it was chaos. From their perspective, in the beginning of the response, all three members of the group shared the sense that there was no single person or group in charge. Although many agencies were on the ground, and they each had their own chains of command, there was no unifying leadership of the crash scene overall. Incident command doctrine would change after the 9/11 terror attacks with the help of lessons learned by the responding agencies. After days of responding on the scene, it seemed to the team that every possible agency had their tent set up in the

Pentagon parking lot, but there was no sense of who had the overall authority.[2] The team went around looking for direction, asking other responders who was in charge of incident command so they could deploy their equipment. They needed legitimacy to begin their work in the active crime scene. Nobody knew who was in charge or could give the group any direction until they bumped into a man who called himself Walter.

Walter was an interesting character in the team's memory. Sporting a construction hat, jeans, and a t-shirt, Walter stood at about 5'10" and had a solid build with dark hair. They got the impression that Walter might not be his real name. They did not know what organization or agency he worked for, but he was official-looking and had medical training. He was searching for a loved one who was in the Pentagon when the plane hit. However, upon arrival, his commander's instinct kicked in, and he was soon wearing a construction helmet and directing people where to go and what to do. Cliff approached him for guidance. He stuck out as a focal point on the ground for the rescue effort, a hub of coordination between the many government agencies involved.

"Who is in charge here? We are trying to deploy telecommunications equipment to locate survivors by cell phone signals."

The man replied, "Come with me," and took them to a van where he introduced them to an agent named Smith. The team wondered if Smith might also have been a pseudonym. Cliff repeated the request to Agent Smith: "We are from the National Guard Bureau (NGB), and we are here to look for people using telecommunications equipment and cell phone signals."

Agent Smith replied, "This is my crime scene, and if you can go in and save lives, go ahead and do it."

That direction was all the team needed to get started with their mission. They headed for the C and D rings, where the last remains of Flight 77 had come to rest.

Pointing at the rubble, Bob saw a wave on the spectrum analyzer. There was a signal!

The team informed the Federal Emergency Management Agency (FEMA) search and rescue team, who then entered the building. They waited anxiously as the team investigated. Their hopes were dashed when the FEMA team returned an hour later and said they found a ringing cell phone on the second floor, but there were no survivors there. Still, the team now knew that their search technology and plan could work, and they proceeded deeper into the rubble with their equipment. They accessed the building at various points but smoldering fires and falling debris prevented them from getting far.

Cliff, Jack, and Bob proceeded in their mission to the C and D rings, joined by the Pentagon head foreman and two of his contractors. They dragged a generator with them. The group plodded through the chaos, through a corridor next to the helipad control tower, trudging through ejected aircraft debris, including fuel, oils, glass, stone, six-to-eight inches of water, and remains of their brothers and sisters in arms. The further they walked, the less RF interference they encountered, and the more hopeful they felt about finding a survivor's signal.

The Pentagon is a five-story structure with strong columns

supporting the second through fifth floors. Those upper floors did not collapse until thirty minutes after the attack, and there are no confirmed records of personnel dying from the collapse. By the time the trio had arrived with their equipment, the initial rescue of personnel had been completed. Ostensibly, all the people who survived the impact had either made it out of the building, were rescued by their coworkers or the initial first responders on the scene, or had perished trying to escape. The fires had been extinguished before the team arrived, although flames periodically reignited from the accumulation of jet fuel enveloping the devastated building. The fire department was vigilant in monitoring and extinguishing these sporadic fires.

The Pentagon's fire system infrastructure had been destroyed by the time the team commenced their operation, so there were no sprinklers to douse the flames. Various items burned, including Kevlar cloth that lined the concrete walls, carpet, ceiling tile, electrical components, etc., leaving behind fiery soot that caked the floor. By the end of the day, the trio's boot soles were all ruined, melted away from walking across the hot spots. The Pentagon was a hazard, and people were talking about bringing in a wrecking ball to level it right away, already giving up hope on finding any more survivors alive in what was now the ruins of this historic building. The team knew that they had to act quickly to complete their mission before any consequential decisions were made. No wrecking ball was used, but the idea floating around was enough to create a sense of urgency among the first responders.

The first equipment problem they encountered was that the spectrum analyzer required 120 Volts AC to operate, but they were in the middle of a cataclysmic disaster area, and engineers had killed all the power. By the time they reached the center of the search area, the foreman and his contractors had departed with their generator. Being resourceful, the team found 500-foot extension cords in a construction trailer that sat outside a recently renovated area of the Pentagon. Through trial and error—and luck—they located an operational data center closet. The door set was busted open and all the Uninterruptible Power Supplies (UPS), were still running. They ran the extension cords together and plugged them directly into the working electrical outlets. That approach worked temporarily, but it was not ideal. Then the team found an operational American Power Conversion brand UPS used to connect all the computers to the backbone. They plugged their spectrum analyzer into the UPS, which allowed them to work closer to the area where survivors might be found.

Finding the data closet enabled them work in the new sector. They subsequently found additional data center closets and forced open their doors. All the equipment in the damaged areas of the Pentagon had been destroyed and using the power sources for their search was a justifiable reason for damaging some of the components in order to utilize their power. The team could now plug in their equipment across the many sectors of the crash site to search for survivors' cell phone signals.

The team continued their search for survivors who were trapped in areas that were blocked or covered by remnants of the building.

There was not a high likelihood of finding survivors in that circumstance, but even the small possibility of saving someone made the effort meaningful and worthwhile. The equipment was heavy. The group lugged it around, through the fourth and fifth corridors, trudging and crawling through the rubble, expended jet fuel, and all the other noxious reminders of the pernicious attack. Their breathing was obstructed and strenuous. Water—as much as two feet deep in some areas—covered much of the debris about 24 hours after the strike, due to the fire department's staunch efforts to extinguish and control fires throughout the first night after the attack.

Hour after hour, Cliff, Jack, and Bob combed through all five floors of the Pentagon, looking for survivors and calling the phone numbers on their list. Parts of the building were collapsing, and they had to crawl at times, going under walls and through entryways to get from one section to another. The spectrum analyzer never showed any signals. The group advanced all the way to Flight 77's fuselage and nose landing gear. This resting place is considered hallowed ground by the trio.

CHAPTER 4

FORTY-FIVE
INTERMINABLE
MINUTES

THERE ARE THOUSANDS OF STORIES FROM people inside the Pentagon on 9/11, and their memories are clear and often painful, as many of their friends and colleagues did not escape.[3]

Many of the service members and civilian workers and contractors at the Pentagon on the morning of September 11, 2001, had been watching the news, reports of the first plane hitting the World Trade Center. The prevailing thought about this was that it was an airplane accident. However, when a second plane hit, people in the Pentagon knew that something else was happening, and as the headquarters for the United States Department of Defense, it would be a long day for them. It was already busy inside the Pentagon, with the various meetings and work that happens on a normal day.

About twenty thousand personnel were inside the Pentagon that morning. One hundred twenty-five of those personnel died during the attack. Fifty-five of the fatalities were uniformed service members, with the others being civilians and defense department contractors. Another fifty-nine people, plus the five terrorists, died on the airplane meaning that a total of one hundred eighty-four innocent people and five terrorists lost their lives in that single attack.[4]

The main area of destruction was the US Army Personnel Command (PERSCOM) area, and the highest-ranking service member killed in the attack was Lieutenant General Timothy Maude, a Vietnam veteran and the army's Deputy Chief of Staff for Personnel. LG Maude was an extremely smart man—"the smartest man I have ever known," according to one colleague. He could reason on many levels, especially analytically, and had a broad knowledge of personnel systems and the technical side of the business, gained from many progressive levels of leadership in the Adjutant General Branch, covering army personnel functions. Working with research consultants Maude created the "Army of One" campaign that replaced "be all you can be." This change helped increase recruitment, which had been dwindling for nearly a decade. That was his part in transforming the army—changing the anatomy of the personnel system and producing a force of soldiers and army civilians with a supportive and effective personnel system. With the change came a new focus on the well-being of soldiers, army employees, and families. His focus included financial wellbeing, health care, cultural and command climate factors, educational opportunities, and recreational opportunities. This transformational leader was 53 years old when he died, leaving behind his wife and two children.[5]

Hundreds more were injured. Miracles saved many from perishing. One new mother brought her son to work because her babysitter was unavailable that day. After the plane hit, she and a group of coworkers safely escaped through a window to the outside, with her son miraculously unharmed.[6] Many led colleagues to safety and returned to help others, while some were just lucky to make it out alive and went to medical treatment areas.

Many of the survivors and rescuers on the scene of a critical incident feel a sense of survivor's guilt, questioning why they lived while others in the same area did not. The saying, "if it is your time to go, it is your time to go" was repeated by many of the survivors.

Survivors who were at the Pentagon on 9/11 recall hearing a "boom" and crashing sounds that jolted the entire building when all one hundred eighty

Clifford Bauman. Photo credit: US Air Force Staff Sgt. Jarad A. Denton.

thousand pounds of Flight 77 hit.[7] Those in the building described it as a bomb, a detonation, a ball of fire, a thunderclap, or an earthquake. Many initially thought that the sounds were bombs going off inside the Pentagon. People on the other side of the building mention hearing thuds, while those nearest to the impact reported a very loud collision, accompanied by a concussive force. No matter where you were in the Pentagon, you felt the reverberations from the impact on the E-Ring in corridors 4 and 5, on the west side of the building. The building went black after the explosion. It was quickly overwhelmed with hot wind and thick, black smoke and fire that spread throughout the west side of the building.

A split second of silent shock followed the impact, then immediately gave way to tense energy. The sympathetic nervous system activated a physiological signal that sent an energy blast throughout the bodies of those present at the scene. Blood left the brain and went straight to the heart. At the same time, formerly bright rooms turned pitch black. Darkness. Clear air was suffocated by thick, black smoke. Mild temperatures were replaced with intense, scorching heat. The stifling air quickly enveloped personnel, filling their lungs with smoke. Trained military personnel and co-workers called out, telling everyone to get low to the ground to minimize smoke inhalation because smoke rises, and being low to the ground could minimize smoke inhalation.

The scene was chaos and destruction inside the Pentagon. Glass windows shattered, strewing hazardous pieces across the floor. Electronic equipment burst into flames. Ceiling tiles disintegrated or caught fire, falling on personnel as they escaped the wreckage.

Fires devoured the oxygen leaving people short of breath. Live electric wires threatened the shocked and disoriented survivors as they tried to navigate to any exit. Desks, office chairs, cabinets, wall decorations, everything that made up the offices had been tossed about by the impact—and some of it was on fire—turning familiar walkways into hazardous escape routes. Survivors recall withstanding the initial shock only to realize nobody around them was alive. Their survival instinct kicked in.

With so many current and former service members on the grounds, their training kicked in, and personnel shifted into survival mode—find an exit now—or first responder mode—look for and help others escape.

The area had recently been refurbished, so many of the personnel who would normally have been working there were temporarily located in other parts of the building. Otherwise, there would have been many more casualties. However, the renovations also made Wedge 1 less familiar, making both escape and rescue efforts more difficult. There were no windows, and the darkness and smoke compounded the difficulties of maneuvering through hazardous and newly rearranged routes to find an escape. Without light, people who knew the area well became disoriented. Crawling on the ground, avoiding debris and flames made even those who knew their work area exits by heart disoriented, as they were blocked by rubble or had difficulty finding their way to hallway doors, which are a maze in themselves. Breathing was extremely difficult. Survivors from this area report having had a very short field of view, less than twelve inches in some places. When they did find a doorway, too often the bright glow of fire beamed from under the door—this would not be an acceptable exit. So, they kept searching, looking for other exits that wouldn't lead them to an inferno. Escape took survivors anywhere from twenty to forty-five interminable minutes, as they crawled, blind and disoriented, searching for exits that did not lead to extreme heat, thick smoke, or other hazards.

Leaders took charge of groups, motivating them to keep low and continue searching for a way out. Groups formed chains, holding on to each other's legs as they crawled, looking for an exit. Survivors report that this gave them hope, as they were part of a group and not facing death alone. The ceiling and walls collapsed in areas, trapping personnel inside the building. Many did not make it out of their work areas. Hope was dashed when hallways were engulfed in flames, forcing survivors to search for another exit. Other exits were blocked, and the only thing they could do was to press on and keep low, searching, hoping to find a way out.

Sprinkler systems were activated in some areas, and smoke cleared, enabling people to see farther and breathe a little easier as they continued to search for an exit. Still, the smoke was black, thick, and deadly. It was a bit clearer closer to the ground, especially in areas where a sprinkler was dousing the floor with water—for as long as the system worked. Many of the sprinklers were damaged by the explosion and stopped working shortly after they had begun.

People climbed out of windows down to the service roads from both the outer E-Ring to the outside of the building near the heliport entrance and the inner A-Ring to the center courtyard of the building. In both locations, they were able to receive medical triage and evacuations provided by medical professionals and other personnel on the scene who were acting in a first responder capacity. Many from the second floor jumped through glass windows to the ground—some finding blown-out windows and others breaking the glass to escape the collapsing building. Those on the ground did their best to catch those who jumped from the second floor.

Others escaped from their office areas through holes in the walls in the C-ring area, leading to the A-E Drive, and then were able to walk or crawl along the stretch of roadway to the courtyard in the center of the Pentagon. Numerous survivors, especially those near corridors 4 and 5 of the E-Ring, had serious burns that required months of surgery and hospitalization. Others lost appendages or had other severe injuries, but they were alive.

Many made it out just in time, jumping or being heaved out of windows into the arms of helpers on the ground below moments before the building collapsed. Many of the personnel who had worked near the area of impact reported surviving when others they worked alongside did not, simply because they had walked away from the outermost wall, the E-Ring, to use the restroom or for a meeting in another area. They believe they were spared for no other reason than fate or chance. Some people lost all of their officemates while they were down the hall or not at work that day. One army office lost all but three of its twenty-eight employees.[8]

"If it is your time to go, it is your time to go," echoes another soldier, surviving his brothers and sisters in service, just by seconds and pure chance.

CHAPTER 5

ON THE OTHER SIDE OF TOWN

AS NEWS OF THE NEW YORK City Twin Towers attacks filled radio waves, Arlington County Fire Department Captain Steve McCoy and his fire crew of Engine 101 were driving to a training course in Crystal City, Virginia—a small enclave of federal buildings and shopping centers just south of the Pentagon. The fall weather was calm—about seventy degrees with eight-mile-per-hour winds.[9]

At 9:37 a.m. American Airlines Flight 77 shattered the quiet of an already somber morning, descending rapidly over Engine 101's horizon. Captain McCoy and his fire crew witnessed the Boeing 757 flying its bizarre course, the beaming silver underside of the airplane reflecting the streets and buildings below. Flight 77 dropped from about two thousand feet of altitude to hit the Pentagon on the ground in just four horizontal miles. The plane struck the building at a speed of over 500 miles per hour.

Captain McCoy's team heard an explosion as the airplane collided with the Pentagon. Black smoke suddenly clouded the sky, spoiling the autumn breeze. The crew did not know where the plane hit, but they called in the plane crash and notified dispatch that it had happened somewhere in the northern part of Crystal City. Without hesitation, every fire engine that heard the radio call rushed to the area. Captain McCoy knew that this was a terror attack, and he told his department to advise the Federal Bureau of Investigation (FBI). Other fire departments in the vicinity responded to the incident too.

A Fort Myer Fire Department foam unit truck was at the Pentagon when Flight 77 crashed. Fort Myer is a historic Army base, going back to the Civil War. It is located next to Arlington National Cemetery, about one mile from the Pentagon. Two Fort Myer firefighters were injured by shrapnel while they were outside of their firetruck, right in the vicinity of the impact. The crew, including the injured firefighters, jumped into action as the Captain, Dennis Gilroy, called in the location to the fire department. As a black plume of smoke filled the air, more Arlington County fire engines and Emergency Medical Services (EMS) teams arrived on the scene to help. The Metropolitan Washington Airports Authority Fire Department was also involved in the response, providing fire engines, foam, and other mass casualty and large rescue vehicles to aid the response.

Arlington County, Virginia, comprises a legion of businesses and governmental buildings. Nearly two hundred thousand residents lived in the county at the time, but many more people commute there for work, travel as tourists to the various memorials, monuments, and other historic sites, and commute from the Reagan National Airport. Although it is the smallest county in Virginia at just twenty-six square miles, and the smallest self-governing county in the nation, it is a busy scene during the workday. More than twenty thousand DoD personnel were at the Pentagon on 9/11, and many more were in the area at the time of the attack.

The attack on the Pentagon was a large-scale, mass disaster, and many agencies worked together in the response. An incident command system provided a means of communication between the agencies and departments involved so operations could be coordinated at the command level. The Arlington County Fire Department was leading the firefighting effort on the scene and led the incident command system. Cliff's team was not officially "plugged-in" to the incident command system and did not know where they fit into the overall response or who to coordinate with besides the FBI connections they made on the ground. Anytime an agent or official of an organization asked them what they were doing, they would give a general reply that they were asked to be there to look for people.

Emergency operations planners do substantial research and planning to establish automatic, quick responses to deal with every type of disaster scenario conceivable, including terror attacks, accidents, and natural disasters. Disaster response planners work with hospitals, businesses, and governmental departments at all levels. The first World Trade Center attack in

1993 injured over a thousand people. Local hospitals were not prepared at the time for that many patients. Now, multiply that number of injuries by twenty-five! Imagine the coordination needed among the incident commander, first responders, and local hospitals and treatment centers to effectively handle the situation.

The incident response at the Pentagon on September 11, 2001, involved many agencies and various individuals and groups. First responders to the attack included fire departments, EMS teams, local hospitals, clinics and other medical centers, law enforcement—including various agencies such as the FBI, Governmental Emergency Management support—and many volunteers like Cliff and his National Guard team that do not fit into any of the other categories.

Disaster response is always led by local agencies, usually the Fire Department for terror attacks. The Fire Chief leads the response. The Fire Chief for Arlington Fire Department at the time was Edward Plaugher. Within minutes of the attack, the Arlington County Fire Department and other agencies were all assembled and operating together, with the Arlington County Fire Department taking command of the incident.

Arlington County Fire Chief Plaugher had established the first local terrorism response team in the United States as a direct result of witnessing the 1995 Tokyo sarin gas attack. He recognized that first response involves hospitals and other medical support, rather than just police and fire departments. Through public and private partnerships, he set Arlington County up to ensure that a first response situation would not be undermined by hospital room shortages or a lack of medical care. Plaugher's terrorism response team, named the Metropolitan Medical Response System,[10] comprised three units: the hazardous materials response team, the medical management team, and the mass casualty decontamination team. Similar response teams now exist in more than a hundred urban areas. Over the years since its inception, the framework has been developed into what is now called the National Medical Response Team.

Chief Plaugher named Assistant Fire Chief James Schwartz to lead the Arlington County Fire Department fire and rescue operations response as the Incident Commander. Schwartz named Chief John White as EMS operations branch commander and Joint Operations Center Incident Command representative.

The FBI's Washington Field Office had activated a command center in response to the earlier assaults on the Twin Towers. When they learned of the Pentagon attack, Special Agent Chris Combs, the FBI liaison to the National Capital Response Squad, joined Schwartz and his team within the local Incident Command as the FBI liaison to the Incident Commander.

The Arlington County government had a Comprehensive Emergency Management Plan outlining emergency disaster operations, which was followed after American Airlines Flight 77 flew into the Pentagon on 9/11. As part of the plan, Emergency Management Team members coordinated disaster response and recovery operations during the immediate timeframe after the attack.

About one thousand of Arlington County's public employees work in traditional first-responder organizations, such as the sheriff's office, fire department, or police department. Arlington county public services at the time included ten fire departments, ten police beats, and multiple hospitals, medical clinics, and urgent care clinics. More hospitals and emergency care centers were within ten miles in nearby Fairfax, Virginia, and Washington, DC. All these public service employees and facilities worked tirelessly on September 11, 2001, and for days afterward.

Arlington County Fire Department personnel searched extensively for survivors among the wreckage. Department leadership supported the firefighters on the scene. Fairfax County Fire Department helped Arlington County Fire Department with the logistical aspects of the response, including personal protective equipment, medical equipment, and supplies.[11] Other organizations joined the effort in finding and caring for survivors as well.

Procuring additional resources and increasing the number of response personnel was difficult because all flights were grounded. However, professionals found a way to help. One medical group drove medical supplies from Texas to a hospital near the Pentagon so surgeons could perform skin grafts. Two doctors performed more than a hundred skin graft surgeries over a three-week period, working shifts of up to sixteen hours a day.[12] Firefighters worked without breaks. Nearby counties supported the Arlington County Fire Department without limit.

The incident response faced communications difficulties. The supporting hospitals did not have emergency response communications systems in place for the multitude of injured persons arriving at their emergency rooms. Hospital staff did not know patients' conditions or what treatment they needed when they arrived. This prevented the hospitals from preparing for the specific injuries of a patient, until that patient was on site.

EMS support initially included twenty EMS teams, as well as two buses and a separate vehicle for the EMS commander, Captain Edward Blunt. Captain Blunt appointed a treatment area in a field at the Pentagon, as well as areas to triage the wounded to be transported to the correct hospital or care facility, based on the severity of their injuries and the capabilities of the various medical resources in the area. Medical support units were assigned to several areas around the Pentagon, as well as in the courtyard, to care for the wounded.

Incident response continued following 9/11. Pentagon staff assembled the Emergency Operations Center (EOC), also called the "War Room," for weeks following 9/11. Staff sections answered calls and responded to requests for information (RFIs) and requests for assistance (RFAs). Colonel Ric Talley—who narrowly avoided losing his life because he took a bathroom break on his way to a meeting—was assigned to the War Room staff. He made his way to the War Room traversing the transportation shutdown to arrive at the Pentagon at 7:00 p.m. daily to develop the upcoming 7:00 a.m. morning briefing for the Secretary of Defense, the Joint Staff, and VIPs. Update briefings at the Joint Staff level convey crucial information put to slides with attention to detail evocative of engineers or architects. Graphics, charts, and graphs tell the story of the state of response by section. The Chief of Staff runs the show and the Executive Officer coordinates. Staff sections in the joint operating environment are notated by J and a number representing the staff section's role: J1 for Manpower and Personnel; J2 for Intelligence; J3 for Operations; J4 for Logistics; J5 for Strategy, Plans, and Policy; J6 for Cyber Operations; J7 for Force Development; and J8 for Force Structure, Resources, and Assessment.[13] In addition to the main staff sections, special staff sections include public affairs (media relations), medical, legal, and liaisons from local and federal agencies, such as DIA, CIA, DHS, and TSA, among others. After the briefing, the staff returned home as the day shift resumed answering RFIs, RFAs, along with coordination and planning duties. The night shift returned at 7:00 p.m. to repeat the process.

Corporate support came in the form of fast-food trucks providing sustenance to the staff. Politicians talked with the families of those who lost loved ones. Thousands of personnel were displaced and worked in Crystal City until July 2002. Operations continued during the investigations and incident response.

CHAPTER 6

THE SON OF A WEALTHY CONSTRUCTION MAGNATE

THE 9/11 TERROR ATTACKS ON THE World Trade Center Twin Towers and the Pentagon are rooted in Afghanistan. The Soviet Union invaded Afghanistan in December 1979, provoking the Soviet-Afghan War. The Soviet army entered to support the communist Afghan government. Afghan guerilla fighters, called the mujahideen, resisted the Soviets and the Afghan communist government, engaging them in a holy war, a *jihad* in the Islamic tradition. Enter Osama bin Laden.

The son of a wealthy construction magnate, Osama bin Laden supported the mujahideen with various weapons and manpower resources. In effect, the al-Qaeda terror network grew out of the fight against the communist Afghan government and the Soviet army. The terrorist group would set their sights on America in the following decades.

Throughout the decade of the Soviet-Afghan War, 1979 to 1989, the resistance's financial network grew immensely. Al-Qaeda was formally established as a network in 1989 to continue the fight after the end of the Soviet-Afghan War. The first leader of al-Qaeda was Abdullah Azzam, and he sought to turn Afghanistan into an Islamist government. Azzam was killed in Pakistan at the end of the Soviet-Afghan War. After arguments between one side, which wanted to focus the jihad on Afghanistan, and another side that wanted to further their jihad globally, Osama bin Laden took over the leadership of al-Qaeda. He believed the group should act well beyond the borders of Afghanistan. The network operated out of Afghanistan and Pakistan but had global intentions. Osama bin Laden was exiled from his birth country, Saudi Arabia, in the early 1990s because of his outspoken criticism of American troops in Saudi Arabia. He and his al-Qaeda network soon focused their terror on western targets with the intention of removing western influences from the Muslim world.[14]

Al-Qaeda's goal was to replace moderate middle eastern governments with extreme anti-American, anti-western governments. They were combative to governments that cooperated with the west. American service members had traditionally never been targeted for violence. Al-Qaeda changed that.

On December 29, 1992, a terrorist detonated a bomb in a hotel that frequently housed members of the American military on their way to Somalia. No troops were in the hotel at the time, but the blast killed two civilians—an Austrian citizen and a Yemeni—and injured others. The terrorists then set their sights on a second hotel in the area, which also often housed American service members. The bomb detonated early, and there were no fatalities. Both attacks failed to meet their objectives, but Osama bin Laden's al-Qaeda, and groups trained by al-Qaeda would become deadlier just months later in Mogadishu, Somalia.

In October 1993, Somali fighters shot rocket-propelled grenades at two American Blackhawk helicopters that were part of a humanitarian mission in Mogadishu, Somalia, killing eighteen US soldiers and wounding seventy-three. The fighters who shot down the two helicopters were not part of al-Qaeda, but they had been trained by the group.

As part of his strategy to defeat western influences in the Arab world, Osama bin Laden sent military subject matter experts to Somalia to assist a warlord named Mohamed Farah Aidid. Al-Qaeda taught the Somali fighters where to aim the rocket-propelled grenades. The attack was a spectacle broadcast worldwide. After the US ended their humanitarian mission in support of the United Nations, bin Laden made statements calling the United States weak for withdrawing after defeat in a "minor battle." He believed years after the attack that the loss left the United States humiliated and defeated. Osama bin Laden and thousands of others—including Somali children—cheered and rejoiced at the killing of the eighteen US soldiers. Although al-Qaeda was only indirectly responsible for the Mogadishu deaths, their fighters would soon be directly attacking and murdering westerners.

Right after noon on February 26, 1993, an al-Qaeda-trained terrorist named Ramzi Yousef and his partner, Eyad Ismoil, drove a rented truck, loaded with a fifteen-hundred-pound fertilizer-based bomb, into the parking garage under the World Trade Center. Yousef lit a long fuse, and they both fled the scene, waiting to see the explosion and the aftermath they planned. The urea nitrate-hydrogen device set off an explosion so big that it left a hole of about 100 feet in width in multiple levels of concrete. Smoke rose up through the building, through the stairwells and elevator shafts, all the way up to the ninetieth floors in both towers. This was a deadly explosion—though not as deadly as Yousef desired.[15]

Many people were trapped in the thick smoke, including a group of small children who were on a field trip and returning from the observation deck in one of the towers. The children were stuck in the tower for about five hours. Six people died in the attack, although the plan was for the explosion to cause one of the towers to crash into the other, killing as many as a hundred thousand people in one catastrophic terror attack. Yousef estimated that nearly a quarter of a million people would have been in the buildings at the time. Indeed, experts later declared that if the van had been parked in a different location, the attack could have been much more deadly.[16]

The mastermind of the attack, Ramzi Yousef, trained at an al-Qaeda training camp prior to his time planning the first World Trade Center attack. Moreover, his uncle, Khalid Shaikh

Mohammed Ali Fadden was one of the main planners of the 9/11 terror attacks, as well as the failed attack on the other target, presumably the White House or the US Capitol Building. Yousef entered the United States with a fake Iraqi passport and requested political asylum in the United States. He was released with an asylum hearing appointment. Another partner, Ahmed Ajaj, traveled with him but was detained over an altered Swedish passport. He was searched and officials found instructions on how to make bombs on him, and he was arrested. Yousef and Ajaj were on the same flight but traveled separately as part of their plan. Once in the United States, Sheikh Omar Abdel-Rahman from Egypt, known as the "Blind Sheikh," connected Yousef to his co-conspirators for the attack. Abdel-Rahman was later convicted of sedition for the 1993 World Trade Center bombing, and he died in a federal prison in 2017.

The largest al-Qaeda attack in the 1990s occurred at the US embassies in Nairobi, Kenya, and Dar es Salaam, Tanzania. On August 7, 1998, two truck bombs exploded at two separate US embassies. The first attack in Nairobi, Kenya, killed 213 people, including twelve Americans. Minutes later, another truck bomb exploded at the US embassy in Dar es Salaam, Tanzania, about five hundred miles south of Nairobi, Kenya. Eleven people were killed in that attack. Thousands more were injured in both attacks, and the massive truck bombs annihilated both buildings and obliterated much of the areas surrounding the embassies.

The East African attacks marked a dramatic escalation in violence from al-Qaeda on Americans as, before these bombings, the terror group had only committed small or indirect attacks against the United States. Al-Qaeda trained terrorists who were not under the order of Osama bin Laden but shared his ideology. They would then attack Americans, such as in the cases of Mogadishu, Somalia, or the first World Trade Center attack.

There would be other terror attacks against western targets between 1998 and 2001, including an October 2000 suicide attack on the USS Cole—a US Navy guided missile destroyer—that killed seventeen sailors. Osama bin Laden's ideal targets were those that represented American international authority and power. The USS Cole was one such symbol, but he had his sights on four other targets the very next year. He chose the two World Trade Center towers, the Pentagon, and an unknown location—ostensibly the White House or the US Capitol building in Washington, DC. The latter choices represent the United States' centralized government and democracy, in general. The flight that had been designated for the last target was brought down by its passengers, and the final target has never been one hundred percent confirmed.

CHAPTER 7

GUYS WITH MACHINE GUNS ARE LOOKING FOR YOU

THE HAZARDOUS AIR QUALITY PERSISTED AROUND the site of the Pentagon attack. Cliff and Bob stayed, while Jack was called back partway through the second day. The building was still filled with smoke, and debris floated in the air. The pair took breaks every hour or so to get fresh air. The Pentagon was flooded. Water and goo poured from every crack, and the FBI gave them DuPont Tyvek brand boot covers and disposable protective coveralls to continue their search. Other first responders asked them where they had received the gear, and they referred them to the FBI command center.

Now, Cliff, Jack, and Bob were volunteer first responders, not attached to any specific first responder group in a statutory sense. When agents or other first responders asked who they were with, they would note their working relationship with the FBI and give them Walter's name. They considered themselves authorized to conduct their operations under the approval of the FBI.

While taking a break for clean air, another first responder approached them with a warning.

"Guys with machine guns are looking for you. You need to keep a low profile. People are asking questions about you running around in your military uniforms with telecom equipment in a building just viciously attacked by terrorists. It does not look good, guys. You'd better get hyper cognizant of where you are and what is going on around you."

Sure enough, the guys with machine guns found them.

Officers wearing creased white shirts, and name tapes, gray pants with maroon stripes and not a speck of dirt on them approached the team. These men were apparently from a federal agency of some brand, not Secret Service, but high in the hierarchy of federal agencies.

"This is an active crime scene of a very serious event. Who are you? What are you doing here?"

The team explained what they were doing.

"Stay here. Do not move."

The agents left. The team's anxiety grew.

"I need to go use the bathroom. I will be back in an hour."

"There are no bathrooms here, Jack."

"Bob, you do the talking, unfortunately neither Jack or I speak English good."

"Neither Jack nor I," corrected Bob.

"See? Exactly why you should do the talking!"

Bob did not have to do the talking after all. Walter intercepted the agents from returning and prevented the three men's arrest. He was their man on the inside who had enough sway on the scene to protect the team and allow them to work. He was their guardian angel, but much later, people would call Cliff a guardian angel.

CHAPTER 8

A DRIVER'S LICENSE, AN AMERICAN EXPRESS GOLD CARD, AND $6 IN CASH

AMERICAN AIRLINES FLIGHT 77 HIT THE outside wall of the Pentagon between the fourth and fifth corridors with such force that the nose of the airplane and a large section of the fuselage plunged through the outside wall and broke through all the way to the C-Ring wall. This created a portal for people to escape and for rescuers to enter. It created a massive, nearly perfect central hole in the A-E Drive wall. Wreckage piled up along the B-Ring wall, from one courtyard to the next. This was the final resting place of the front-most tip of the airplane, a marker to the amount of force with which the Boeing 757 hit the Pentagon.

The landing gear likely blew off the plane and landed separately, totally intact at the C-ring. They created an astonishing spectacle, like the closing sequence of a *Looney Tunes* cartoon when Porky Pig pops through the hole—"That's All Folks!" Many people were able to escape through the hole, as traditional doorways or openings were not accessible because of fire, obstructions, or damage. Cliff and his team were in that area for three days, entering and exiting through the A-E Drive portal. This area in particular upset all members of the team. Days were spent walking around body parts, all tagged with blue flags by the FBI. Annihilation. Stress. Trauma. Anger. Cursing.

Bob ran across an auxiliary power unit fuel gauge at the landing gear site and picked it up. The glass was broken, but it was still covered in aluminum and easily identifiable as the fuel gauge of Flight 77. He put it back as it was part of an ongoing investigation. All three of the team were professionals, and they knew they had an ethical duty not to disturb or remove anything from the site. They continued their journey through the Pentagon. Walking. Crawling. Spotting a shoe or another clue that may lead to a possible survivor buried in the area. Investigating. Calling the same cell phone numbers over and over again. Pointing the antenna in different directions and hoping for signal spikes on the spectrum analyzer.

The trio endured, climbing around the wreckage and chaos, picture frames broken on the floor, walls collapsed or riddled with holes, debris piled on top of other debris, acting as stairwells leading to other areas to search. The hazardous conditions of the building caused them to change their search methods. They determined it was best for two to search at a time, while the third waited on the outside in case an area collapsed and the group became trapped. The young men focused on the first and second floors, between the third and fourth corridors. The higher floors had collapsed within the first hour after the attack.

During their work, the team encountered other personnel who were also searching for items, gathering documents littered by the explosion, or performing different investigations for various agencies. Often, they heard: "What are you doing here? You should not be in this area! Get out of this area immediately!" After explaining, they were allowed to continue each time.

What they were doing looked unusual to the other first responders and investigators, and after they stated their clearance to be there and explained their methods, the others would ask them to call various phone numbers. They called the numbers each time, but never got any signal on the spectrum analyzer that might indicate the phone was active in the sector. It was a continuous process of searching, explaining, and dialing. After making calls for the other agencies and first responders, the teams would separate and return to what they had been doing.

Throughout the first day, the FBI established a strong presence in the command and control of the situation. Although Incident Command was the Arlington Fire Department, the FBI on the ground was very visible and helpful with direction. The team fell under their command and worked alongside them. The National Transportation Safety Board (NTSB) also had agents working the incident response. Cliff and Bob overheard NTSB agents talking about finding the black box. The term "black box" is colloquial and refers to the original color of the case containing the aircraft flight data recorder and cockpit voice recorder. The box itself is now fluorescent orange to make it more noticeable in the wreckage after an airplane accident. Cliff walked up to the NTSB group talking about the black box and inquired how much water was required to activate it. The group replied that it took 18 inches of water to initiate the tracking "ping." Cliff informed them that there was more than 18 inches of water in parts of the Pentagon.

Bob had subject matter expertise with Air Force capabilities and told them to call over to Andrews Air Force Base, sixteen miles away, and ask for a black box detector. The NTSB listened to Bob and called base operations at Andrews, but they were unable to send the equipment at that time. Workers located the recorders at about four in the morning on September 14, three days after the attack, at the point of initial impact. The NTSB retrieved data from the flight recorder, but the cockpit voice recorder was in poor condition.[17]

The group took turns going into the crash site through the A-E Drive portal made by Flight 77's nose. To Jack, walking down the fuselage's final resting place felt like he was walking down the aisle of the plane. They walked through the devastation. One of the rear landing wheels, which was torn in a straight line, resembling the side of a donut, but otherwise intact, survived in the wastage. Many bizarre sights still reverberate with the group today, many years later. After seeing an agent looking for folders earlier in the day, Jack noticed what he thought was a folder under a brown seat cushion. He walked over to investigate. It was not a brown seat cushion. It was a torso with a brown shirt. He and Cliff believe it was the torso of one of the hijackers on the plane. The memories of the tragedy enrage Jack to this day. He is not alone.

The search continued. Bob noticed something intriguing at the wheel well. It was an eel skin wallet, untouched, not wet, not covered with anything—just sitting there with the rest of the debris. Bob picked it up and saw a woman's driver's license, an American Express Gold Card, and $6 cash. He handed it to Jack. Jack handed it to Cliff. Cliff looked through the gray wallet, reading her name, Norma Cruz Khan, age 45, from Reston, Virginia. Norma was a Puerto Rican and had been married to a Pakistani man. She had an infectious smile, a kind heart, a sense of humor, a love for life, and a deep love for her thirteen-year-old son. He was inseparable from her. She was the Manager of Member Services for the National Plumbing-Heating-Cooling Contractors Association, headed to Reno for a business trip.[18]

Norma Cruz Khan did not like to travel because it separated her from her son. A neighbor gave the news to her son. He went to live with another family member who, coincidentally, was a pilot for American Airlines. Those who knew Norma say they feel the pain of losing her every day. Cliff, Jack, and Bob looked for Norma in the building. Cliff believes he saw her, but Jack and Bob do not recall if she was one of the victims they encountered. The group put the wallet back on the wheel well, respecting Norma and the active crime scene, but they would remember

Norma forever. Her name, her face, and the remarkable condition of her gray, eel skin wallet—the most pristine, stainless artifact in all of the wreckage of American Airlines Flight 77, deep in the C-Ring of the Pentagon ruins.

CHAPTER 9

YOU'RE NOT GOING ANYWHERE

BOB HEWETT IS A RATIONALIST. HE knows how to deal with things effectively. He wanted to avoid getting too involved in the human or emotional aspect of the response. He was there to do a job, and he follows the army mindset of mission first, people always. Bob used his technical knowledge during the three days, doing his best to help others through technical problem solving. Hour after hour, new challenges popped up to keep Bob occupied. There were emotion-provoking scenes, deceased soldiers, airmen, sailors, marines, and civilians throughout the ruins, but at the time there was nothing they could do to help them anymore. That was the reality of what happened, and they were there on a mission. Concentrating on the challenge was a coping skill Bob used in the moment of the response, a mindset that helped him get through the tragedy, a way to keep his focus and perspective. Of course, they all had a punch in the gut going into the B and C rings of the Pentagon, seeing the center of the carnage, the last testament of American Airlines Flight 77.

The day after the attack, after reporting to his boss with an After-Action Review of the previous day, CW2 Jack Du Teil asked to return to the scene to continue the effort of the day before.

"No, you're not going anywhere."

The lawyers were now involved. Although in the heat of the moment, the team was free to respond and save lives, legal involvement and implications for responding became more prominent after the initial shock and hasty planning and response. Now these implications limited what first responder and recovery operations military leadership would approve. Nevertheless, Cliff and Bob found themselves back at the Pentagon, resuming their important work.

CHAPTER 10

MIRACLES HAPPEN IN SECONDS

CLIFFORD BAUMAN SHOULD HAVE DIED ON September 11, 2001. His boss—a Lieutenant Colonel—came in late to work, so they were behind their normal departure time from the NGB building to report to the Pentagon. Cliff, then a Chief Warrant Officer 2, the Lieutenant Colonel, and another soldier were a block away at 9:37 a.m. when Flight 77 hit the west side of the Pentagon at the center of the Army Personnel headquarters—exactly where they were supposed to be at the time.

This trio joins a long list of people who escaped fate that day for various reasons. One senior army officer had just left his cubicle in anticipation of a meeting that he predicted would take place due to the attacks on the World Trade Center in New York City. Walking away from his section toward an elevator, he heard a great big boom, and everything went dark. He led people from other sections out of the area, saving many lives. His friends and coworkers in his section did not make it. "If it is your time, it is your time," he says. Many other survivors of traumatic events express the same fatalistic sentiment. Miracles are counted in seconds.

Clifford Bauman. Photo credit: Alia Dastagir, USA Today.

Another senior army officer, Colonel Ric Talley, recalls how his "small bladder" saved his life. He was an army aviator and a public affairs officer who had just finished Army War College in Carlisle, Pennsylvania, preparing him for a senior leadership role as a brigade commander. This would be his last position before retiring. At least, that is what he thought. He did not know the Army's plans for him, or for that matter, fate's plans for him. He was in a "holding pattern" at the Pentagon as he waited to relocate for his new position and was temporarily assigned as Director of Media Relations for the Army. The morning of 9/11, he was busy and barely aware of the people watching the news and talking outside his office. He tuned in for a minute and watched a news report of a commercial airliner flying into one of the twin towers in New York City before he had to march off to a meeting.

"That's impossible. I'm an aviator; no air traffic controller would let anyone get near there," he remarked.

At 9:30 a.m., he walked from his office in the E-Ring, second floor, to the D-Ring stairwell, down to the D-Ring, first floor, toward the PERSCOM wedge, to coordinate a meeting for Media Day. A major renovation had just been completed on the PERSCOM wedge, and there were barely any personnel there, compared to normal operations before the renovation. He recalled how drawn-out previous Media Day meetings had been and decided to use the bathroom before the meeting started. He turned around and walked back up the stairwell to a private one-stall bathroom. At 9:35 he retraced his steps down the stairwell, through the D-Ring hallway, to the PERSCOM wedge. That short delay in reporting resulted in him being outside rather than inside a demolished conference room.

The ground shook, like an earthquake. He stopped in his tracks. Debris of white, powdery, crushed sheetrock rained down and wafted, clouding the hallway air. A maintenance cart carrying boxes of folders shot through an open door and flew past him. The powdery sheetrock rapidly turned denser, covering him. He heard screams as panicked coworkers ran from the PERSCOM wedge. *This must be a helicopter crash or a propane tank explosion*, he thought. Whatever it was, he knew he needed to vacate the point of impact. He ran up the stairs, thirty feet to the E-Ring, second floor, and joined a group that was doing the same thing he was doing—escaping death or serious bodily injury from the burning building.

Speed walking with a group of colleagues, he linked up with a three-star general he knew.

"Ric, what happened?" the general asked.

"I don't know, sir."

Ric scanned the area for a clue and picked up a piece of metal, examining it as he moved. It had a thin, visible aluminum oxide coat, indicating that it had gone through the anodizing process, an important step in preparing metal for use in airframes. Anodizing metal adds resistance to the corrosion that results from dissimilar metal contact and exposure to elements. It stops metal from returning to its original form—rock, iron ore, etc. He was familiar with that coating from his experience with helicopter airframes.

"I think this is possibly part of the tail boom of a helicopter."

The artifact confirmed his initial suspicion that it was a helicopter or another small aircraft that did the damage. He put it down as it could be evidence that the DoD, FBI, or TSA would examine later in their investigation. Along with the twenty thousand others who were inside the building, he walked toward Arlington Cemetery, just a mile northwest of the Pentagon, as the crow flies.

Now out of the impact zone, Ric and the lieutenant general turned around to see what they had escaped from. Orange fire and thick, billowing black smoke curled to the sky. At one point, someone over a loudspeaker called for any able-bodied personnel to return to the building to help bring out the wounded. A group of about one hundred personnel did an about-face, turning back to the Pentagon and running back to the devastation. They had just about reached the building when they heard another announcement: "STOP. Turn around and continue away from the Pentagon."

The group listened to the command and resumed moving away from the Pentagon. The order was ostensibly due to intelligence of a possible second attack. If so, it likely alluded to another hijacked airliner, United Airlines Flight 93, whose target was never fully determined, though it was likely destined for the White House or the US Capitol.[19] Hundreds gathered under stone bridges that cross the George Washington Memorial Parkway and run alongside the Pentagon. Many were injured and being cared for by others.

Ric departed the holding area and started walking to his home in Old Town, Alexandria, Virginia. He walked under the I-395 bridge, to the Pentagon City Mall, and on to the Pentagon City Metro Station. All lines were shut down. He walked to his Alexandria townhouse, arriving just before 1:00 p.m. He had thirty-seven voicemails, but he did not return any of them save for a call to his parents. Just hours later, at 4:00 p.m., the Pentagon called.

"Report as soon as possible to the Emergency Operations Center Media Desk."

He responded, "It's still on fire!"

He reported, nonetheless. He would be part of the Pentagon Emergency Operations Center for the following weeks.

In the summer of 2002, he finally left the Pentagon to take brigade command.

Timing and chance determined the fortune of many service members and civilian defense department employees. The accounts of personnel assigned to the areas most damaged by Flight 77 subsumes many stories of fortunate employees being away from their desks because they were out of the office for temporary-duty assignments, traveling for official business, attending medical or other appointments, or taking time off for vacations at the end of the fiscal year.[20]

Jack's best friend should also have died on 9/11. Taking care of an administrative task on the other side of the Pentagon saved his life. Jack knew that his friend worked in the area where the plane struck, and he knew that almost nobody in that section survived. He tried to call him but could not get through. Returning from the Pentagon after a day spent searching the rubble for survivors, he cried because he firmly believed his best friend was dead. By pure chance—or a miracle—his friend lived. The officer returned to duty immediately after 9/11. He and Jack served together in Iraq following 9/11, and they both retired years later after serving honorably in the War on Terror.

Another story that shows chance's underlining force in fate involves an army officer and his infant son. The child started daycare that very day in the Pentagon Day Care Center. The man dropped his son off early in the morning before going to work on the other side of the building. Daycare workers recommended that he help ease the transition by visiting every hour for a couple of minutes, then going back to work since he worked in the building.

"Doing that will let them know you are here, and it eases the daycare transition."

The man left his office to visit his child just before Flight 77 hit the Pentagon that morning. He was returning to his office when it crashed right into his workspace. He would have died instantly if he had been sitting at his desk at 9:37 a.m. His kid saved his life.[21]

The NGB was originally located in corridor three of the Pentagon but had been relocated to Jefferson Plaza 1 during the renovation. If they had not been temporarily relocated, they would have been right in the center of the devastation where the belly of Flight 77 rested. All National Guard leadership could have been killed but for the opportune timing of the renovation in their sector in the Pentagon.

Cliff felt guilty for surviving the attack when so many others did not. He is part of a long tradition of heroes and survivors haunted by the memories of living through an event where others died. Many survivors miraculously escape death, only to struggle with the pure randomness of being alive, and developing severe guilt. Many survivors later attempt suicide to rid themselves of this guilt. By not seeking help for their Post-Traumatic Stress Disorder (PTSD) and retaining strong feelings of "survivor's guilt," a survivor can turn against themselves and join the ones they outlived through suicide. In a sad, unnecessary mental affliction, the circle is complete for them. PTSD and survivor's guilt has taken the lives of high school shooting survivors, law enforcement officers, survivors of vehicle accidents, and witnesses to tragedies.[22] They survived deadly situations physically intact, but emotionally undone. As Jack Du Teil says, "The human brain is a very complex computer."

This complex computer of our minds runs various programs called coping mechanisms that determine what each of us will do in a situation. Like our genetic makeup, all of our coping mechanisms are unique to us. They have been shaped not only by biological heredity, but also by previous experiences—success, failure, and past trauma. Emotions become tied up in our memory of events, which affects how we process and react to future events. Some survivors have positive coping mechanisms, such as trying to find the good in everything. Others have harmful coping mechanisms, such as self-blame. Positive and negative coping styles and strategies are not mutually exclusive, as there is a time and place for both.

Some potentially positive coping mechanisms can actually be bad. For instance, being overly positive and denying the bad elements in society might help a person believe in a just world, but it is also a denial of the malevolent elements around them. They may be easily victimized, as they are not in touch with their sense of danger. Ignoring something does not make it go away, and you can potentially lose situational awareness if you are in denial of danger. On the opposite side, some negative coping mechanisms can be helpful. For instance, focusing on what you did wrong in an event can negatively affect your well-being, but it can also help you learn from the experience and prepare you for future events.

The circular steps of experiencing an event, reacting to it, recovering from it, and preparing for another event is called a "feedback loop." Each event teaches us something new and prepares us to face similar events in the future. The learning should happen while we are recovering from the event, and optimally, we should adapt and learn rather than take on new coping strategies that do not prepare us for future events.

PTSD prevents us from learning and growing as first responders and people. We want our coping mechanisms to help us make sense of events and deal with them in a positive manner. We want to find the balance between the reflection and introspection following an event that helps us deal with it positively and the need to retain the event's true characteristics in our mind to learn from it without getting caught up in the negative emotional experiences. We do not want an event's memory to prevent us from progress. Instead, it should effectively change how we prepare and respond to future events. There is a feedback loop that takes the effects and outcomes of events and changes how we prepare for similar events, should they happen in the future.

Each of us use different mechanisms to keep focused and keep going. You could say we all run different software. In responding to the Pentagon on 9/11, Bob focused on the technical aspects. It helped him deal with the task at hand. Cliff was determined and committed to keep going while there was any slight chance of rescuing someone alive in the rubble. Jack was angry and driven. He knew soldiers who worked in the area, good friends who had likely been killed.

Sometimes our survival mechanisms or self-defense mechanisms lead to irrational thoughts and behavior. The minds of all three first responders were running different programs in the aftermath of 9/11, and it affected the path of their lives from that day. Cliff developed what Jack called an irrational feeling of guilt about not finding anyone alive. The group found many dead people and body parts from dead people, but they did not locate any survivors; they were not able to save anyone. Cliff's guilt was irrational because they had no control over the situation and finding any survivors would have been based on luck alone—not on anything the group did or did not do. But Cliff subconsciously believed they had some level of control. Survivor's guilt relies on the survivor believing the outcome weighs more on their actions than on fate or anything out of their control.

Survivor's guilt explains a single part of the syndrome responsible for first responder and survivors' suicide attempts. Without the capability for physical self-harm, there would be just thoughts of suicide. The capability for suicide is acquired through experiences, including witnessing traumatic events such as the mass murder tragedies of terror attacks and mass shootings. In witnessing such events, we lose our sensitivity to life versus death.

People in certain professions are more likely to witness the results of violence and thereby become less sensitive to it. Therefore soldiers, police officers, emergency room doctors, paramedics, and others who witness grave injuries in the line of work have more acquired capability for suicide than people who are not regularly exposed to trauma. Survivors of extremely violent events, such as 9/11 or the Parkland shooting, would be more capable of suicide simply because of their familiarity with death and trauma. Without treatment people like Chief Clifford Bauman or the two Parkland students who died by suicide shortly after the shooting could have the disposition in them to attempt suicide. And if their suicide attempt fails, the habituation and acceptance of self-destruction as an act by suicide attempt is strengthened, making subsequent attempts more possible. Many soldiers, shooting survivors, or others who have experienced great violence are at an increased risk of self-destruction and suicide. Survivor's guilt is irrational, makes a person feel like they are a burden to others, and is influenced by a person's childhood relationship to the world around them. It needs to be addressed if we are serious about fighting suicide.[23]

Understanding that fate really is a chance set of outcomes that circumstance picked for us—and that we had no part in the choice—could be a good frame of mind for someone struggling with survivor's guilt. Is believing that you are the center of the world and all things, good or bad, rely on your personal alchemy a healthy mindset? Such magical thinking leaves us susceptible to survivor's guilt. Would having a mindset that you are just a small part of the big picture, and you really have no control at all over many situations be a better way to think about things? The question regards empowerment versus guilt. Being in control of all outcomes, including deadly ones could lead to guilt, while leaving all outcomes to chance might leave you feeling powerless to change anything. What is the right amount of control over events we should feel? And how do we get there?

Our relationship with the world around us can give us some answers to that question. What survivors and those who feel like a burden[24] to others need is to see the view from the outside their own perspective—to be shown how much they matter. Asking the right questions can lead a person to insight on their relationship with others and the world around them:

"Are you really a burden to others, considering all you have done for those in your orbit?"

"How much of a role did chance play in the event you are stuck on?"

"What would things look like for others in your life if you were no longer around?"

"What advantages do you provide for those around you?"

"Now, tell me if you still think you are a burden to those around you?"

This is the line of questioning that can lead to insight and lead someone away from guilt and suicide. However, just a fleeting insight will not take away the self-blame or self-destruction forever. That requires more sessions with a skilled therapist or counselor who can walk with you on a journey through your mind, a quest for life-giving insight; for that is the gift of a good clinical psychologist, therapist, counselor, etc. Their talent is in helping you think outside what is on the surface to find out what lies beneath and to gain an understanding of your own value and your deepest self.

CHAPTER 11

WHAT WOULD THAT PERSON WANT YOU TO DO IF THEY WERE HERE IN FRONT OF YOU RIGHT NOW?

NOT ALL PEOPLE DEAL WITH DIFFERENT experiences in the same way. In fact, the different ways in which we deal with negative events really is the determining factor for how they impact our lives. Every event means different things to each person who experiences it. What would happen if we all dealt with the same situations in a uniform way? Things would be predictable. Yet, things are not predictable. The only thing predictable is that our reactions are *unpredictable*.

Survival depends on finding ways to live through negative experiences. Letting something that happened to you dictate your life and speed up an instinct for self-destruction is irrational. Perhaps it is an archaic or primordial part of our nature. Feeling sincere respect and sympathy for someone you were actively trying to save has its place. However, letting that memory and its clinging sense of loss absorb you can have negative consequences. Respect and sensitivity should not be an affliction. Through counseling, Cliff Bauman discovered a way to turn pain and a heartfelt devotion to memories of the victims into a powerful positive force from which to help others. He emerged from his life's trauma with significant damage, but found a way out of it, able to learn from his experience and grow in strength and empathy rather than let it destroy him.

Leaving behind those that did not survive events we responded to and moving on, never looking back, is an impossibility for many people. Coping with first responder experiences can take many forms. Some people experience "compassion fatigue" and lose their sensitivity to others as a coping mechanism to protect their own mental health.[25] Police can find themselves doing this if they respond to people in numerous emotional situations. Other helpers can become overly sensitive, taking on others' stress as their own. Psychologists often do this, and it affects their mental health. A good balance, as stated by many first responders, is to find a way to deal with the trauma in a way that works best for you, but always keep a professional face on the job. Compartmentalizing your work and private life, and keeping your empathy, your sanity, and your professionalism when dealing with situations would be the greatest developed mindset we could achieve. Now, this may require effort to maintain such a mindset if you are constantly working through events where you put everything you have into helping others.

People who have survived traumatic, deadly events often experience depression, anxiety, and other natural but dysfunctional emotions.[26] These emotions can get in the way of human development and obstruct one's path to living a full life. Previous research has focused on survivor's guilt in the context of Holocaust survivors, first responders, people who grew up in poverty, and other groups who survived what many of their peers did not. Adults who grew up in poverty often experience survivor's guilt when they experience success in their lives, while those they grew up with never got the same chance.[27]

The first thing that survivors need to do is to understand what their thinking patterns are, including where they come from and how they affect their lives. They must then find ways to deal with the things that cause them stress. If you are a friend or family member of a survivor or a first responder going through these emotions, you might be the best person around that can help them recognize that they need help and encourage them to reach out to a professional who can help them. Therapists, counselors, and other professionals can develop interventions to help your friend or family member. For Cliff, it was the depression of not finding any survivors that caused his distress. For other survivors, it will be something else. But the irrational and dysfunctional coping manifestations of PTSD and survivor's guilt will result in stress of some kind. When the stress gets to be too much and the first responder starts to think about suicide, they are experiencing a crisis where they need to find a reason to live.

The search for the meaning of life is part of the "human condition," a term that describes all the events and features of human life (birth, spirituality, family life, physical health, death, etc.). The human condition entails human suffering throughout life, along with all the positive things that happen in our experience of the incredible miracle that we are alive as sentient beings. Many thinkers have written about the meaning of life and finding reasons to live, but one of the most well-known is modern psychiatrist and Holocaust survivor, Viktor Frankl. He believed that we should find meaning even in our sufferings. How many times have you heard someone say that suffering makes us stronger? Frankl takes that cliché and gives it depth and definition as both a philosophy and a form of psychotherapy.[28]

Courageously facing the human condition and all its adversity head-on and finding meaning in it is our journey. Sometimes the suffering is not physical in nature, and often for first responders and other survivors, it can be guilt for not having done more or not being able to save someone, even when they had no control over the outcome. We can support those struggling through this guilt by helping them reach some insight about the event in the context of the meaning of life. For example, shifting focus away from the first responder's sense of guilt and putting themselves in the shoes of a victim to consider what the victim would want the survivor to accomplish with their life can lead to insight and a reason to live. Viktor Frankl's psychotherapy is called "logotherapy." It is based on the foundational premise that life is worth living, and the therapist must listen attentively for the side of *life* of the person talking to become clear. The therapist would then phrase things in such a way that the survivor finds insight in their story and a reason to go on living—even thriving.[29]

Humans need to have a sense of what they have accomplished in their life, as well as a sense of what they have not done yet but wish to do. The hope of completing something, being a part of something, or changing something they are not happy with is a major source of life for us. Often when people are angry about something, it is because they wish circumstances were different. Their anger at the current state of something is essentially a major driving force upon which they can focus their energy—be it anger, frustration, or hopelessness—on a reason to live. Because they are angry, we know they are passionate about something. Finding their reason to live can refresh their life. Helping them find it is our mission.

In his book, Frankl presents his brand of psychotherapy, called logotherapy, derived from the Greek term *logos,* which translates to "meaning." He declares that the chief impetus motivating human beings is the drive to find a meaning for life. The poignant memories and philosophical reflections of his time spent in the bleakest existence imaginable as a prisoner in a concentration camp guided Frankl in the development of logotherapy.

If a concentration camp prisoner can find a meaning in his life, then we should know that our situations are survivable. There is depression as things happen to us, but Frankl declares that there is always meaning. The focus of logotherapy is to find our meaning of life and then find a way to live. Cliff's story is true, and many good people died. His team did not discover any survivors in the ruins of the Pentagon. However, by digging deep to answer the questions posed to him by his counselors, he thought about things in a new way, taking the valuable lessons and a drive to help others, rather than to complete self-destruction.

Logotherapy is not about developing coping mechanisms to help people live through their struggles, it is about accepting the struggle and finding meaning in it and using their energy to be productive in their struggle.

Humans find meaning to life in many ways, including faith in God, spirituality, social relationships, travel, accomplishments, memberships to organizations, support for specific causes, and beyond. Becoming an adult involves finding your purpose and your meaning. This search gives us focus. People who have lost the meaning in their life can be at risk of many negative things until they find that meaning once more. What people need then, is a reason to live. Frankl found his reason in the most miserable of conditions. Cliff found his reason to live years after going through a very stressful, traumatic, and guilt-provoking experience. Others can find a reason to live too.

So, now it is time for application. Here are some questions: How can we help another person find meaning in their life? Does it happen by giving solid advice or by listening and asking follow-up questions? Does the reason to live come from the counselor or from the person themselves? If it comes from the person, why is that the case? Now, these are not regular questions, they are Socratic questions. And these questions can lead us to the answer of how we can lead others to insight about their own reasons to live.

The Greek philosopher Socrates invented a method of teaching through asking questions before 400 BC.[30] Socratic questioning is used in many fields. In education, it can be an excellent teaching method when a teacher wants to engage students and help them reach their own conclusions, as opposed to the didactic approach where the teacher stands in front of the students with a slideshow or a chalkboard. An instructor can direct their students to valuable insight in a way that has them arrive at the answers and discover insights on their own. It is a very valuable way to acquire knowledge, and the lesson learned lasts longer because the student came up with it themselves. Insight from Socratic questioning is ingrained into the mind in a different way than information that is simply taken in from outside sources. Socratic questioning is used by counselors and psychologists as well.

We will not dig into all the therapeutic techniques used by professionals during interventions, but we will describe how logotherapy applied through Socratic questioning can help someone find a reason to live. It can enable us to help a friend, patient, family member, co-worker, etc. gain insight into their personal story and find a meaning for their life. And logotherapy through Socratic questioning has been found effective in treating PTSD. [31]

Socratic questions force a person to go deeper into their mind for buried insights. They challenge their assumptions and back up their ideas with facts. Or they realize something is not valid, and they determine where they should go next. The counselor is a guide to help them look at the past from different angles, to learn from their past by looking at what they would change if they were to repeat an experience, or why it is important to feel like they do and come out with insightful lessons. It is about finding meaning, a drive, and a way to achieve what is in their conscience. Conclusions and insight come to the surface, and they get to see what is triggering their thoughts, attitudes, feelings, and frustrations.

When clients, loved ones, coworkers, and others have an epiphany and an insight into something about their life and suffering, the meaning of their life becomes apparent. The energy is palpable—both the counselor and the counselee can feel the life force focus and strengthen. Imagine finding the true purpose for your existence. Envision the spiritual awakening someone overcome with survivor's guilt feels when they start to let go of the unnecessary guilt and focus on a way to make it all better. Now, see yourself helping another person find this in themself. The spiritual force can be contagious and helping a person find a reason to live, a purpose to guide them might become part of the meaning of *your* life. Some Socratic questions regarding this lesson: Can being a part of this, as a counselor, ignite the search for meaning in our own lives? Can helping others rediscover their passion for life be a purpose in our life? Why or why not?

Now we will go over some useful lines of Socratic questioning to help others. Some questions you can use to guide the dialogue and help your friend or family member find insight could include:

- "What did you learn from this intense experience? What would you do differently if you were in that situation again? How can you apply what you learned to make the future better for yourself and others?"

- "What makes life worth living for?"

- "What does your emotion (frustration, sorrow, etc.) tell you about yourself? What can you do to use that emotion to make a difference?"

- "How are your current behaviors honoring, memorializing, respecting, and paying tribute to those who were lost? What behaviors would honor their legacies better than what you are doing now?"

- "What would that person want you to do if they were here in front of you right now?"

- "What would your best life look like?"

- "Does what you are doing advance your core objective? What would advance it?"

- "Do you blame other first responders that have lost people? Is it proper to blame yourself if you do not blame them for the same situation?"

- "Do you believe in second chances? Do *you* deserve another shot? What would your parents/children/friends say to this question?"

- "If you end your own life, who wins? Who loses? How can *you* win?"

- "Do you really deserve the death penalty for your actions? What penalty do you deserve? How much of the sentence have you already served? Is it time to end your sentence now?"

- "What did you want to accomplish before taking on survivor's guilt?"

- "Would your battle buddy want you to live your life and accomplish your goals? What would honor them? Furthermore, how would they feel about you being so loyal as to take on the responsibility for their misfortune when it was merely chance?"

- "How can you make the world a better place by applying what you learned from this experience?"

Exploration of the meaning of life and how to live are gifts to our friends, family members, patients, clients, etc. Finding a reason to live and the motivation to keep going is just the start though. Our friends now need to learn how they will follow their goals in the face of difficulty. It is one thing to fixate your mind on meaning, but another to energize your spirit to live with hope and purpose. So where do we go from here? From the example questions above, if our friend stated that if the person they tried to save were speaking to them at this moment, they would want them to know that, although they could not save them, they would want to be remembered by teaching lessons to other first responders in how to save others in the future. Then they would need to find a way to do this. Let us develop that reason a little more. A counselor could then ask, "How can we memorialize that person and let their spirit live on through the lessons taught to other first responders?" The next answer might have to do with different methods in taking the past situation and creating a book, video, pamphlet, training guide, etc. for first responders to be knowledgeable and capable of supporting others in the same situation. Such a product could save many lives! So going from frustration and guilt over an event in their past to finding meaning and helping others is a product of the therapy session or deep conversation with a friend going through problems.

The meaning of life is so personal to each of us. We cannot guess what it is for someone else. That is why asking questions is so important. By coming to their own conclusion of why life is worth living, the reason becomes personal, even spiritual. Our role is to guide them there as a therapist or a listening friend.

The ways in which our friend can apply the insight from our Socratic questioning session—going deep into not just an event, but the frustrations and lessons, then eventually hope and meaning for the future—originate from a trained and caring family member, friend, or counselor who digs deep with them on the overwhelming thoughts and feelings that have latched onto their experiences. Imparting insight, energy, and hope for the future leads to a drive to change their future. It must be remembered at all times, though, that the counselor is a facilitator for insight—not a director, but a guide in the quest for purpose and meaning that can lift someone from the depths of trauma and despair. Our role is to help the survivor gain their own insight and direction through the use of questions, and not by getting too close to the story. This course may take many conversations and requires a deep exploration of inner values and a person's purpose for living.

If you have provided counseling according to this method, you have helped another person find meaning in their life. To make solid this new commitment to a reason to live, you can examine different ways to keep this change forever in their mind and in their spirit through follow-up conversations or counseling sessions, depending on the nature of your relationship with them. The person in discussion may want to post reminders of their focus on purpose. Journaling or making lists of actions that will lead to finding their reason to live. Writing books or creating music or art to focus on their individualized quest for meaning can all be helpful. Writing down plans that will lead to their ideal life or tracking triumphs and victories that are part of their mission also support this evolution of their life.

Whatever it takes to substantiate the insights from each discussion on finding a meaning to live, there should be some next step in place to help keep their insights in mind for when the inevitable slump comes and finding meaning in life becomes necessary again. You may have to repeat the process with them multiple times to reinforce their commitment to life and to their constant search for meaning in it. In the end, you are empowering the person through affirming their life and journey toward purpose. This is how helping someone move beyond survivor's guilt works, and the same methods also help with suicide prevention.

In life-threatening incidents, it is chance that determines who is injured or killed. We usually have no say in the outcome at all. So why would we blame ourselves for something determined by circumstance? It can be difficult for a veteran or a survivor to come to this conclusion when they have the inward-focused predisposition to blame themselves. Even with an "aha!" moment of insight, the verdict of innocence can be short-lived. Both psychotherapy and the therapy with Socratic questioning have this same limitation. Deep insight can be forgotten, and old habits take over. In much the same way as addiction works, the inner mind's self-blame and self-harm habits are at the center of the person while they are alone in their mind. Long-lasting change and strategies to deal with this inner predilection for self-blame or self-harm must be dealt with through therapy. A belief that the mind can be permanently changed by some insight does not consider the predispositions of our minds. The insight must therefore be at least an understanding of ourselves and not a new way of living. It would be amazing if a single insight could forever straighten our paths, but we must accept that the greatest outcome of self-discovery is to begin to see that there is a possibility to become free of survivor's guilt, self-blame, and self-destruction; changing this in reality requires long-term counseling, or psychotherapy if the self-blame is deeply ingrained.

CHAPTER 12

A GLITCH IN THE SYSTEM

CLIFF EXPERIENCED THINGS THAT DAY THAT he didn't realize would impact him later. The sights, sounds, vehicles, concrete pillars, the weather, uniforms of all the service members and agents, the ambulances, helicopters, water, smells, the mortal remains of brothers and sisters. They didn't seem important at the time, but they intruded upon his memory later at unexpected times. They became triggers to his PTSD.

PTSD is an identifier used for diagnostic classification purposes into a category called "Trauma and Stressor-Related Disorders" in the American Psychiatric Association's Diagnostic and Statistical Manual of Mental Disorders, Fifth Edition (DSM-5).[32] PTSD is a disorder that confounds a person's connection with reality. It can lead them to altered states of thought: dissociation, depersonalization, derealization, pareidolia, and apophenia. PTSD can lead to a glitch in the mind. What you think is reality is not. And it is all traced back to trauma.

The tendency to see patterns that do not actually exist is called apophenia. It is a glitch in the system that can convert just about anything into a PTSD trigger. Immaterial details seem to relate to your trauma, and everything is accorded a deeper meaning. It is all connected somehow, your mind tells you. It is an ageless trap, a paranoia that is doing nothing good for you. It has done nothing for anybody.[33] It may actually be the root of many superstitions throughout history, and it is often based on someone's previous trauma.

Pareidolia is another glitch in the system that can relate to past trauma. Pareidolia is seeing something that is not there. The man on the moon. The face on the planet Mars. A cloud shaped like an Olympian. With PTSD, it is another way your mind is wreaking havoc on your emotions. The shapes that somewhat resemble something they are not. There is everyday pareidolia, and there is PTSD pareidolia—attaching false meaning to an event. The meaning is an illusion as nothing is actually connected; the event was random and driven by chance. But it takes on a meaning in your mind. Then there is survivor's pareidolia—attaching fault when none was there. Survivor's guilt would fall under this umbrella. Fabricating personal responsibility when there was no way to alter the outcome. Assigning responsibility when there was nothing but circumstance. Shifting what you perceived you could control. The mind, overthinking and full of random thoughts, attaches recriminations when there are none. Trauma and stress lead to anxiety. An anxiety disorder makes us feel like something is worse than it is; a muscle spasm is a fractured bone, an upset stomach is stomach poisoning, a friend who is running late is probably in trouble. In pareidolia, everything that happens is given greater significance than it deserves, and we have to constantly be alert, doing or thinking the right things to keep control of our psyche. Everything is a warning. Everything is a harbinger. Another trap that puts our minds back into a previous trauma. Pareidolia manifests innocently enough with objects, but it is a Trojan horse for total control of the psyche. Intrusive thoughts must be internally confronted. PTSD leads to strange thinking.

PTSD symptoms are common in an initial screening after responding to a critical incident, but they generally improve with time. Within a couple years most symptoms disappear altogether for the majority of responders. Moreover, many first responders to large-scale disasters do not develop PTSD at all. That fact is a testament to the effective intermediate and advanced training and general resilience of our first responders.[34] Possibly some people do not have a predisposition for PTSD.

First responders experience a range of traumatic exposure, and some responders witness or experience trauma at higher levels than others. If the first responder does develop PTSD, it resolves itself over time in most cases. However, some research has found that World Trade Center non-traditional first responders contin-ued to experience PTSD symptoms many years after the attack. Symptoms tend to last longer for volunteer respondents to an event, like Cliff, than they do for traditional first responders, like police officers and firefighters. Symptoms vary by the nature and scale of the event, the person's exposure to the trauma, and how the first responder was prepared for the event. People who act as first responders but are not trained as first responders experience psychological challenges such as depression and PTSD at a greater rate than those who are trained first responders.[35]

Many agencies screen for PTSD directly after any traumatic incident, but PTSD can have a delayed onset of symptoms. Since first responders frequently aid in traumatic situations, continued screening is important for first-responder agencies and organizations. High-risk personnel can be referred to treatment—a crucial step because many people will not seek it on their own. They are not naturally help-seekers. Having a strong screening and referral program in place can ensure high-risk employees get the help they need to maintain their emotional well-being. Cliff Bauman had to learn to seek help the hard way, through his own journey that almost took his life.

CHAPTER 13

YOU DON'T THINK TWICE ABOUT WHAT YOU SAW UNTIL YOU DO

PTSD IS DEEPLY SET IN HUMAN history. It is a group of symptoms countless people throughout human history have faced after surviving traumatic situations. Trauma, including war, domestic or personal assault, natural disasters, major accidents, and other serious events, has been part of the human condition forever and will be until the day the last human is gone from the world. It would not be a stretch to say that PTSD symptoms have affected humans in all areas of the world, throughout our history. In our modern day, behavioral scientists have classified PTSD as a set of symptoms with their negative effects on a person's life, in combination with a prerequisite traumatic event. Mental health professionals have used such titles as "shell shock," (World War I), "combat fatigue" (World War II), and at present PTSD. The symptoms are not exclusive to those who have fought in a war. Any person can find themselves involved in a traumatic situation, no matter their career, lifestyle, wealth, or any other factor; however, military members and first responders are at a higher risk of experiencing such situations.

Trauma survivors with PTSD focus part of their lives in the past and are not completely living in the present. This comes in the form of intrusive thoughts, emotions, dreams, or nightmares. They are detached from others around them and their immediate environment. To avoid being triggered, persons suffering from PTSD will often avoid people—including close friends and family members—or scenarios that remind them of the traumatic event that is hanging over them. This helps them keep a distance from it. The survival mechanisms playing out in the mind may work in the wild when facing actual danger, but they are irrational when there is no present danger.

PTSD definitions and diagnoses are continually updated as mental health associations and experts adapt to their patients and address their needs. The predominant authority on PTSD diagnosis is the DSM-5. This fifth edition was released in May 2013.[36] The nature and level of the experience of a traumatic event was changed between the fourth and fifth editions.

In the fourth edition, "The person experienced, witnessed, or was confronted with an event or events that involved actual or threatened death or serious injury, or a threat to the physical integrity of self or others."[37]

However, in the DSM-5, the authors expanded the event characteristics to include many more types of experiences, rather than exclusively facing death or serious injury. In the new version, you can be diagnosed with PTSD if you were a bystander, or even if you were not physically present at the traumatic event.

The text reads, "You were exposed to one or more event(s) that involved death or threatened death, actual or threatened serious injury, or threatened sexual violation. In addition, these events were experienced in one or more of the following ways: You experienced the event; You witnessed the event as it occurred to someone else; You learned about an event where a close relative or friend experienced an actual or threatened violent or accidental death; You experienced repeated exposure to distressing details of an event, such as a police officer repeatedly hearing details about child sexual abuse."[38]

Indirect exposure to an event is now regarded as traumatic enough to warrant a PTSD diagnosis. Examples can include police going through old cases, airmen observing drone aircraft attack footage, paramedics and doctors performing routine operations and activities, etc. Other frequent outcomes of being a first responder to a large-scale terror attack include major depressive disorder, substance use disorder, generalized anxiety disorder, and panic disorder.[39]

The intrusions into your psyche can manifest through psychological or emotional anxiety brought on by symbols of the event, or even physiological or physical responses to these internal or external reminders of the traumatic event. This can include unexplained body aches and pains, exaggerated startle response to noises, an overtaxed pulmonary or nervous system, the inability to relax, and all the accompanying issues caused by each of these reactions. PTSD is not just a mental or emotional reaction; it is a physical reaction as well.[40]

A PTSD diagnosis comprises more than simply a symptomatic reaction to an event. The term "disorder" refers to an interruption of normal functioning. Post-Traumatic Stress *Disorder* then infers that there is a negative effect caused by the earlier traumatic stress.

Humans naturally avoid situations and places that they do not like. Memories are no different. PTSD compels people to avoid reminders or stimuli of a traumatic event. It necessitates an internal exertion of energy to avoid a thought pattern, feeling, or memory from the event. Psychological maneuvers like this are stressful as they require the denial of something you have no control over. Your mind shifts into high gear to fight off memories. Doing this for extended time periods takes your mind off your current situation and taxes your mental resources.

Another type of avoidance is the palpable and external. You will physically avoid people who were present at the event, the place where it happened, or even a place that is similar or reminds you of the experience. You may try to stay away from situations that might trigger the memory or avoid various activities, or even conversations, if they represent a risk to your psyche.

PTSD is a common repercussion of surviving a catastrophe. Furthermore, PTSD is more prevalent after terror attacks than it is for other manmade and natural disasters.[41] Many first responders to the 9/11 terror attacks on the World Trade Center and the Pentagon dealt with PTSD for years afterward. Different studies found varied durations of 9/11 first responders' PTSD symptoms. One study showed that about 11 percent of first responders to the World Trade Center attack had PTSD symptoms five years after the attacks.[42] Another study found that ten years after 9/11, 15 percent of the first responders registered in a health-tracking database had PTSD symptoms.[43] There is a trajectory with PTSD, meaning that it fluctuates between increasing, decreasing, and remaining stable in severity. The fluctuations differ between individuals based on personal characteristics, risk factors, protective factors, and exposure.[44] According to another study, PTSD for first responders peaks five to six years after the event.[45] However, PTSD symptoms normally decline in the following years. PTSD is most significant right after a disaster, but for many people, its onset is delayed, with symptoms showing up months, even years, after the triggering event. A study about Pentagon workers found that PTSD rates climbed in Pentagon staff in the months and years following 9/11, with about 8 percent of the staff developing PTSD in the first four months following 9/11, 14 percent in the seven months following 9/11, 23 percent in the 13 months following 9/11, and finally declining to 16 percent in the 25 months after 9/11. This study focused on all personnel and staff at the Pentagon on 9/11, not just the first responders.[46]

The rates of PTSD are increased for the people who are not traditional, specially-trained first responders.[47] Researchers found that the PTSD rate for police officers, firefighters, and other trained responders who assisted after the World Trade Center attack on 9/11 was about six percent at two and three years after the attack. However, the rate for volunteers doing first-responder work, but not attached to the police department, fire department, or other agencies or organizations was more than three times higher: about twenty-one percent.[48] A similar study found an increase in PTSD of almost four times between police and non-traditional first responders at the World Trade Center after 9/11.[49] Other workers, mostly from construction, engineering, and utilities backgrounds, had a PTSD rate of about eighteen percent in the same time frame.

Researchers find that there are different outcomes for traditional first responders, such as police officers, firefighters, detectives, sergeants, law enforcement command staff, sheriffs, state troopers, constables, paramedics, etc. when compared to other nontraditional first responders who were at the scene and helped simply because they were in the right place at the right time.[50] Police officers and other first responders get specific training to deal with critical incidents. They get extensive tactical first aid training, including how to stop massive bleeding, how to clear an airway obstruction, and how to treat a person who has stopped breathing. Good Samaritans often do not have this training.

Commuters and residents in the area, many of whom were not first responders nor trained in disaster response, witnessed trauma, death, injury, and physical and emotional suffering. Furthermore, a many of them had the initial trauma of being in danger of losing their lives. That is why first responders' PTSD rates are higher than those of the general population, but lower than those of survivors of traumatic events. The survivors that first responders help score higher on PTSD symptoms compared to the first responders and are more likely to experience PTSD than their rescuers. Different studies report different statistics, but overall, first responders PTSD rates do not reach the high levels seen in survivors of terror attacks and other deadly, traumatic disasters. There are different qualities to the different levels of exposure to trauma in the DSM-5 diagnostic criteria.

However, it must be stated that people in the general population are not exposed to disasters as much as first responders who routinely run toward peril in their line of duty, so the likelihood of developing PTSD is higher with the first responder group. The difference is that PTSD rates for first responders who are not accustomed to or trained for working in these traumatic situations is distinctly higher than those who are in the line of work as a profession. Why is this the case? Does the training first responders receive prepare their psyche for responding to such events and witnessing trauma? Is it because people who tend to work in the first responder fields have a different personality make-up, including strong coping methods for dealing with trauma? Might it be that many traditional first responders have PTSD but they keep it a secret? Perhaps police officers and fire-fighters are trained to recognize the symptoms of PTSD and are able to seek help earlier and more proactively than others. These are all reasonable explanations for the differences in susceptibility to PTSD for those in first responder careers, versus the volunteers who become first responders based on circumstance, such as Cliff and his team.

Many of the traditional first responders to 9/11 received treatment through their employers as part of a screening and care process. For others, such as Cliff Bauman and his team, there was no screening program. They also had no organizational debriefing sessions that could have helped to mitigate potential PTSD down the road. In most cases, when PTSD affected a volunteer responder, they had to get help on their own, often urged by friends and family members who noticed warning signs.

Cliff fell into this group, suffering from PTSD and under risk of causing harm to his physical, emotional, and spiritual self before he finally sought treatment. It was a miracle that he survived the risks and his suicide attempt.[51]

Surviving any traumatic event may lead to experiencing PTSD symptoms. The first warning sign is the re-experiencing of the traumatic event. This can come in many forms. Thoughts and memories from the experience can intrude into your mind through basic memories, or as flashbacks or nightmares. These intrusions into your psyche can be vivid as you can re-experience sights, sounds, and other sensory reminders. It feels like you are actually reliving the event. Nonetheless, these memories are not productive or rational, as they occur during normal situations that are not related to the event and do not cue a *rational* survival need.

For example, the light snow on the ground in Northern Virginia during the winter may bring back memories of the blinding sand of a Middle Eastern war zone, but there is no reason to take cover should you hear the buzzer of your friend's cell phone. And there is no reason to break away quickly when another car follows too closely on the freeway years after using your defensive driving on a highway in Basra, Iraq. The scenes may seem familiar, but the situation and the dangers are not the same.

CHAPTER 14

THEY WOULD NOT TAKE IT BACK OR DO ANYTHING ELSE

CLIFF JOINED THE ARMY NATIONAL GUARD with his brother Chris and two of their friends, Troy Galloway and Steve Harper. The group attended weekend drills with the 1106th Transportation Company in Aurora, Missouri, just across the street from Aurora High School, which they attended. Drills took place in an old boiler room in the basement. It was an enjoyable time for Cliff and the group as they made a lot of friends and a lot of great memories.

They did goofy things to make it fun. Their unit, G Company in the 135th Aviation Regiment of the Missouri Army National Guard, often went to Germany for their annual two-week training. Since Cliff and his older brother Chris were both Sergeants at the same time, they had a running joke that when a supervisor asked them to do a task, they would reply, "You told the other Sergeant Bauman to do that, not me!" It was quite funny to them.

Cliff's brother Chris went on to join the Reserve Officers' Training Corps at Southwest Missouri State (now just Missouri State) with his friend Troy, leaving the unit to become commissioned officers. Chris served for 20 years altogether and retired as a Captain. Troy stayed in much longer and was promoted to a two-star general in June 2019. His two daughters also became commissioned officers, one attending The United States Military Academy (West Point) and serving as an army officer, and the other going to The Merchant Marine Academy and serving as a Merchant Marine.

In 1996 Cliff decided he wanted to become a commissioned officer. He applied and was accepted to the Warrant Officer program. He left G Company in July 1997 for Warrant Officer Candidate School (WOCS), in Fort Rucker, Alabama. That is where he first crossed paths with Jack Du Teil. They knew each other as classmates in what Jack called the "army's worst school." WOCS was a very high tempo course, with training seven days a week for eight weeks straight. There was no time for making friends, but they recognized each other years after the course and would become colleagues and friends.

Jack will forever remember Cliff as a very skinny soldier. Cliff, at that time, was slim, but athletic, and was the physical training officer for the class. After the course ended, everyone went their separate ways without building deep friendships during the short, fast-paced WOCS training. The schools warrant officers attend after their initial training are longer, up to ten months. Cliff stayed in the aviation field he had served in as an enlisted soldier, going from an enlisted Aircraft Armament Repairer to an Aviation Warrant Officer. He was at Fort Rucker, Alabama, for the aviation school, while Jack, a self-described "computer geek," attended a follow-on course at Fort Gordon, Georgia, to become a Data Processing Warrant Officer. The two reconnected when they were both assigned to different sections of NGB. Neither of them had any idea that within a short time they would be first responders together at one site of the biggest terror attack in our nation's history.

A "first responder" is a person who goes into a scene immediately after an accident, attack, or natural disaster to assist the people impacted. First responders are usually professionally trained to deal with situations, although, in unexpected and oftentimes deadly events, personnel without specific job duties or training, or even volunteers in the area, can act as first responders. Generally, we think of police officers, firefighters, emergency medical technicians, SWAT teams, lifeguards, and other designated professionals as traditional first responders. However, a major event can turn anyone into a first responder. Non-first responder personnel or the general public in the area act as first responders, committing their energy to assisting others on the scene. The attack on the Pentagon was one such occasion where there were many non-traditional first responders involved in rescue attempts.

First responders experience others' trauma and tragedy. It is in their job description. They are crucial during deadly events, but being in the first responder line of work entails its own sacrifices. PTSD is a widely accepted consequence of first response careers.

The DSM-5 criteria for a PTSD diagnosis includes firsthand, direct exposure as well as many other secondhand experiences like witnessing death or serious injury, finding out that a person close to you has witnessed death or serious injury, or even indirectly being subjected to hearing specific pieces of information from traumatic situations. First responders are routinely exposed to trauma in all these ways.

One commonly experienced example of PTSD from indirect trauma exposure would be police officers handling bodies after crimes. Their lives were not in danger when handling the body or bodies, but the exposure to the results of the trauma, according to the new criteria, may leave them vulnerable to PTSD symptoms. Of course, this example is not the only time when police officers deal with trauma, as they routinely experience and witness many types of violence and tragedy throughout their careers. The situations dealt with by police officers can affect them in multiple ways. The psychological consequences of being exposed to years of trauma can affect first responders through PTSD and various other psychological, occupational, or physical impacts.

Police officers can go from a traumatic scene to a routine scene in the same hour at work. They must be professional, not showing any hint of the harrowing things they see. Blocking emotions helps them to be professional at all times in the interests of the people they are responding to. They must have a command presence—an outward projection of authority. This demeanor is essential to police officers for the reasons above. One might assume that all law enforcement must be born with a sense of command, and that they self-select their careers based on their own personality and skills. That is often not the case. Police officers join the force for various reasons—reputation, respect from the community, financial stability, or childhood dreams, to name a few. They come into the police force with different personalities and skill sets. Many do not have an intrinsic commanding presence. However, it can be trained in the police academy or gained through experience and mentorship. The presence and professionalism they develop over time helps them keep them impervious to breakdown and emotionally bulletproof. It is a necessity of their job.

By the time a police officer has been in their career a decade or so, they can expect to have been shot at, threatened with knives, and in vehicle pursuits. Most are involved in or present at multiple deadly-force situations during their careers, be it ten years, twenty years, or longer. Police officers need to de-escalate a situation rather than escalate it, which can make the difference between having their lives threatened versus resolving issues peacefully. However, there are situations where de-escalation is not possible and when they face violent persons who will do whatever it takes to remain free.

Another type of training also helps first responders be successful in dealing with crises. Crisis Intervention Training teaches police officers, military, and other traditional first responders how to recognize warning signs that at-risk people may show that they are depressed or considering suicide.[52] They learn to recognize warning signs and how to engage persons at risk of suicide. First responders use their listening and conversation skills, attending to and hearing what the person is saying, and trying to connect with them and get their mind off suicide. They de-escalate the person's emotions calmly, avoiding triggering words, and engage them respectfully. Police officers and other first responders use "verbal de-escalation," which is trained at the police academy. Persons at risk of suicide are often wound up, and the police officer talks with them and calms them down.[53] They may try to connect by asking their name and then using their name. They listen and fish for something the person is willing to talk about which may lure them away from their suicide intent.

Bystanders have saved countless lives, including police officers and firefighters. Police officers would prefer that bystanders do not put their lives in danger, but they absolutely appreciate their support when they can offer it safely. When a bystander responds to an event, they are exposed to that single incidence of trauma. On the other hand, traditional first responders are exposed to situations like this day-in and day-out. It becomes routine. So it makes clear sense that, overall, traditional first responders are more likely to experience PTSD symptoms than the general population. However, non-traditional first responders, victims, or others who are exposed to an incident are more likely to be affected by a single incident and are at risk of developing PTSD from being unprepared to deal with a traumatic situation that a traditional first responder is trained for and experienced in dealing with.

CHAPTER 15

THE "REPTILIAN" BRAIN TAKES OVER

THE GRITTY WHITE SAND PELTED THEIR faces passing through the sides of their goggles and into their eyes, making them wince. Thin grains of sand set off loud, buzzing smoke alarms, and the soldiers bounded for cover from the sandstorm. Reminiscent of being on the ground near a helicopter as it takes off, their instincts were to cover their faces and put their heads down, away from the rotor wash—although this was a large storm, and the sand and debris came from all sides. The soldiers did not know how long this storm would last or what large debris would whack them. So they stayed covered and waited until it passed. The fusion of deadly, unpredictable weather, indirect fire attacks (rockets and mortars), and being in a combat environment created a heightened alertness response in Cliff. However, at the moment, he was not in Iraq, and it was not the year 2007. He was in Wisconsin, and the year was 2020. And there was no sandstorm.

As he spoke to soldiers and airmen of the Wisconsin National Guard, Cliff stared off into the Wisconsin winter hailstorm. A vivid memory of the Iraqi sandstorm occupied his mind, and he had to pinch himself to remember where he was at that moment—to fight the feeling that he was in life-threatening danger. Thirteen years after the initial event, Cliff still dealt with unpredictable flashbacks to the many traumatic situations he had experienced in Iraq. And nearly twenty years after responding to the Pentagon on 9/11, the memories still invaded his present-day life, activating the ancient physiological fight-or-flight system that prepares us to deal with deadly situations. The problem is that the current situations are almost always not actually deadly.

With PTSD, the programmed responses to reminders of actual deadly experiences affect present-day, non-deadly events that contain reminders—or triggers—of the earlier trauma. While reacting appropriately during deadly events means the difference between life or death, escalating the perceived danger of common events wastes physiological and mental resources and creates anxiety. Confounding the severity of events makes everyday life difficult for persons suffering from PTSD. They have difficulty classifying situations correctly as life-threatening versus non-threatening when ordinary experiences and events converge with previous traumatic incidents, putting the mind in high-alert mode. PTSD causes excessive reactions to situations based on imagined threats. Our brains store memories of our experiences at a neural level, in nerve cells that communicate with other nerve cells through chemical and electrical signals.

During events, including traumatic ones, our brain cells are changing to encode information about the event. The emotions and reactions of the previous event, now stored as a lesson for how to deal with the same event when re-encountering it, can carry the mind and body away from the present and back into the past.[54] Living with PTSD involves dealing with triggers, never knowing when they will show up.

The human brain is composed of three parts: the cerebrum, the cerebellum, and the brainstem. The cerebrum constitutes the largest part of the brain and is divided into left and right hemispheres, and each hemisphere is divided into four lobes: frontal, parietal, occipital, and temporal, each with their own functions. The cerebrum carries out higher-level functions, including regulating emotions, coordinating fine motor control, reasoning, problem-solving, decision-making, planning, cognition, self-awareness, hearing, and vision. Areas of the cerebrum oversee sensory connections and emotion regulation, managing emotions to keep them under control so our other brain areas can function and do their job. This part of the brain helps us avoid making bad decisions! The cerebrum also contains components involved in memory consolidation, learning, and behavior. Under the cerebrum lies the cerebellum, and under the cerebellum lies the brain stem. As we go lower, the responsibilities for brain processes in the areas become more base and automatic.

The cerebellum is much smaller than the cerebrum in humans and is responsible for coordinating larger muscle and body movements. The brainstem connects the other two parts to the spinal cord to relay signals throughout the body and executes all the automatic functions we take for granted, such as breathing, our heartbeat, food digestion, and deep sleep cycles.

The limbic system is a cerebral (outer brain) system that coordinates memory, learning, behavior, and emotions. Having those functions in the same system impacts how memories are encoded during emotional situations. Within each hemisphere of the cerebrum, inside each temporal lobe, lives a small, almond-shaped structure, called the amygdala. There is one on the left temporal lobe and one on the right temporal lobe. The amygdala directs our reactions to stimuli and identifies threats. It also attaches emotion to memory. These functions are important to PTSD. What could happen if the part of the brain that identifies threats and initiates alert functions for survival is also the very same part that encodes memories and associated emotions into our brain cells? Is it possible that it can program our fight-or-flight nervous system responses as an over-reactive response system by interconnecting stimuli from past trauma to current environmental cues as perceived threats? Hypervigilance symptoms of PTSD relate to the impact emotion has on memory encoding. When traumatic stimuli of past events get muddied with new events that have some similarity or semblance to the traumatic event, we can be left in a hyper-vigilant state, scanning the environment for threats in an irrational heightened response condition. Now, let's talk about that.

Located between the cerebellum and the brain stem lies what is often called the "reptilian brain," or "old brain." It comprises many smaller structures important to survival. The autonomic nervous system residing in the old brain is an important component to survival as it controls both our fight-or-flight response and our recovery response. Two parts of the autonomic nervous system include the sympathetic nervous system, which is responsible for fight-or-flight responses, and the parasympathetic nervous system, which controls recovery operations after responding to a threat. During stressful situations, the lower-level, ancient reptilian brain takes over from the higher-level cerebrum tasks. The lower brain initiates the fight-or-flight response by way of the sympathetic nervous system releasing hormones to drive survival actions. This reaction requires a lot of energy and blood flow, and it takes resources from the higher-level brain systems, essentially shutting down higher-brain functions to deal with an immediate threat. After an event is over, the parasympathetic nervous system kicks in and decreases stress hormones to bring more blood to the other brain systems, restoring the brain and body back to equilibrium. For the most part, that is, as there are exceptions.

If the transition from the reactive sympathetic nervous system response to the parasympathetic restore and reset mode does not take place, as often happens in cases of PTSD, a person can be at a heightened, or susceptive, status when they should be going back to normal functioning, encoding the memory in a way that teaches them how to survive a similar situation in the future. Instead, they are encoding emotion to the memory, which will not help them survive future threats. This relates to the hypervigilance mentioned above. In this manner, our brains biologically change with traumatic experiences as new memory cells adjust how we respond to corresponding, and seemingly interchangeable, experiences. Consequently, a brain with PTSD operates divergently as a result of a traumatic experience. However, the same way your brain learned an irrational function, it can learn sensible functioning again through the same system.[55]

CHAPTER 16

I WILL NEVER DO A SLEEP STUDY AGAIN!

DURING LARGE COUNTERINSURGENCY OPERATIONS, SUCH AS the ones in Iraq and Afghanistan, the United States and Allied Forces capture large areas to use as their base of operations. They become relatively safe locations to work out of, often including counter artillery apparatuses to protect from many of the rockets and mortars fired at them indirectly. Leaving the safety of the base is termed, "going outside the wire." There are many reason service members go outside the wire, such as for operations, transportation of logistics, investigating crimes and leads on terrorists, coordinating logistics or intelligence with local leaders, and to recover casualties, lost crew, and vehicles. Tragically, aircraft, especially helicopters, crash or get shot down in war. Recovering the crews and the wreckage is dangerous, but Americans do not leave comrades behind. And they take calculated risks to recover sensitive technology and information from crash sites.

The year was 2007, and Cliff was part of a hastily formed helicopter recovery team that had a mission outside the wire. The soldiers were excited to be doing something new after being inside the base for so long. Their convoy departed to recover a helicopter in the Iraqi desert. They were outfitted with special gear, including wires connected to their head and body. The wires were uncomfortable, and it was a feeling Cliff would encode in his memory cells. The team arrived at the wreckage site and set up a perimeter to guard the area while they operated to secure the crew and equipment. There he was, working inside another disaster zone. Memories of 9/11 were activated on a cellular level, and he was alert. Rightfully so, as the situation and area was dangerous. The team worked through the night, and he never got fully accustomed to the wires attached to his head and body. It was especially uncomfortable at night, in the pitch black. A new memory was encoded, as the pitch black of the night and the constant irritation of the wires commingled with the danger of being outside the wire with a small team in a combat zone. The new memory cells were tagged with the sensory stimuli of the gear he was wearing, the stimuli around him, and the wreckage. The encoded memory could show up years later, if triggered.

With the wires attached to his head and body, it seemed strange to be laying down in such a dangerous zone. Cliff started sensing that things were not right. He didn't feel his helmet, only wires. And where was his uniform? Where was his team? He screamed. The long pitch-black night was cut short abruptly by the fluorescent tube light on the ceiling. He was in a hospital room.

There was someone outside the door. Again, he pinched himself to bring his mind back to the here-and-now. The sleep doctor entered the room. It had been another flashback. "I will never do another sleep study, Doc!"

Sleep is essential for humans' physical, mental, and emotional health.[56] Indeed, many first responders experience sleep disturbance problems. Cliff experienced difficulties getting quality sleep due to his PTSD and nightmares. First responders experiencing PTSD symptoms sleep less, on average, than the rest of the population. The quality of their sleep is not sufficient to make them ready for work the next day. This

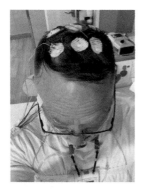

Cliff at his sleep study. Photo credit: Clifford Bauman.

further exacerbates their PTSD symptoms and the negative effect they have on the person's social and occupational life. People in other professions also have trouble getting enough sleep, and it correlates significantly to difficulties in other areas of their lives. Soldiers with sleep problems are much more likely to experience risk factors for suicide.

Sleep can help regulate reaction to trauma both before and after an event. If you do not have enough sleep *before* responding to a traumatic event, then you are at a higher risk of developing PTSD or other difficulties such as substance use or depressive disorders. On the other hand, if you sleep directly *after* a traumatic event, you experience fewer flashbacks, nightmares, stressful thoughts or memories, and less anxiety when triggered by analogous or seemingly comparable situations. So, if you sleep well before or after a traumatic event, you will not be as affected by it versus if you do not sleep well, and you will be able to process the experience better in the long run. However, many first responders do not sleep well, and that can leave them susceptible to stress, PTSD, anxiety disorders, and other problems. Even after PTSD treatment, many first responders still experience sleep issues.

The quantity and quality of first responders' sleep is lower than that of the general population. Half to nearly three-quarters of first responders experience sleep disturbance.[57] Moreover, first responders who respond to critical events have an even lower quality of sleep and more nightmares than those who respond to non-critical events. However, deadly encounters and other critical events are not the only types of experiences that can affect sleep quality and quantity. Other negative experiences, such as bullying, sexual harassment, or physical altercations, can lead to problems sleeping, but currently scientists find that critical incident exposure is a stronger predictor of a sleep disorder. Cliff had dealt with numerous other negative situations in his life, but he had never had a sleep disorder until he developed PTSD.

Employees with mental health issues such as PTSD miss significantly more days of work compared to employees without those struggles.[58] The avoidance symptoms of PTSD lead to occupational problems, including increased missed days of work.[59] Ostensibly, PTSD treatment would reduce the number of missed days of work and increase work productivity for organizations with a lot of personnel that suffer from PTSD, such as police departments, fire departments, and certain military units.

CHAPTER 17

IS THIS RATIONAL?

POLICE OFFICERS GO THROUGH SCENARIO-BASED TRAINING to prepare them for encountering situations they will face in their field. They go through active shooter training many times during their career. The idea is that when they encounter a real-world active shooter situation, they have repeated their response many, many times and have actions planned out. They should then automatically follow the script and respond effectively. In the crawl-walk-run training system, they will automatically go to "run." They will not need to search for the right response, their muscle memory will take over.

Training for reacting to stressful events can help performance and lessen the risks of emotional involvement. Muscle memory is a powerful tool for training someone to react under stress but being too automatic can lead to failure as well. Imagine being in the middle of a fire fight. You are focused on shooting at a moving target, who is also shooting back at you. You have done this multiple times in a simulation trainer. Your magazine is out of ammunition. You release the magazine, load a new magazine, and then bend over to pick up your spent shell casings. After you pick up the brass shell casings, you put them neatly in a metal container and then proceed to return fire once again. Is this rational? It is an example of how rigorous, inflexible training leads to irrational actions during stressful encounters, and this exact scenario has happened![60] So, how do we train for flexibility and rationality in stressful scenarios?

By incorporating scenarios with varying nuances to enable critical thinking, we can create scenario-based training for real-world events. Police and other first responders need to exercise critical thinking while under stress when the blood is in their heart, not their brain. This requires special training. Our goal is to be quick and accurate with our hand-eye coordination and tactical skills, but to also have situational awareness and an adaptability to deal with the nuances. Police officers must know the right response, while still thinking during the process and adapting so they are not doing anything inefficiently.[61] From the example above, they would be accurately shooting, but leaving their spent brass shell casings on the ground until the fire fight is over! They would not be pausing to clean up their spent ammunition shells in the middle of a fire fight or calculating their shot accuracy—or doing anything that belongs in firearm training but not in real-world events.

Police forces utilize scenario-based training to prepare officers for accident investigations that involve serious injuries. Officers to take command of the scene, direct others, and protect all people at the accident site. Their training prepares them to deal with fluid, ever-changing situations. It leaves them with a basic understanding of what can and will happen during their job duties. When officers encounter such a situation their first time in the real world, they have been through it many times in simulations and can take command confidently and help calm people down.

Our memory encoding is impacted by the effect of brain activity and the dynamics of situations and stress. The human brain's prefrontal cortex is a structure covering the front part of the brain, which facilitates executive thought. It helps us make logical and clear sense of events happening around us. During traumatic experiences, the prefrontal cortex is often offline, replaced by lower brain functions. This affects how memories are encoded or stored for long-term recollection. Consequently, calming a person down during a traumatic event has a positive effect on their memory encoding.

Critical incident response is part of the job for all soldiers, sailors, airmen, marines, and coast guardsmen. Warfighters have dealt with threats to their lives since the very first battle. What have we learned about mitigating PTSD throughout the ages? The answer is Critical Incident Stress Management and Traumatic Event Management.[62] For decades, the military and first responder fields have known that debriefing personnel involved in traumatic and stressful events helps them gain a shared understanding of what happened and helps facilitate the healing process. It also helps them learn from an event to better prepare for future events. Behavioral scientists call this cycle of experiencing trauma, debriefing, learning, and preparing for the next critical incident a "feedback loop." In the uniformed service, and other first response organizations, the term for the debriefings is termed the After-Action Review.[63]

Police forces practice critical stress debriefings after traumatic events, such as officer-involved shootings. In a critical stress debrief, the officer meets with a psychologist or other mental health professional immediately and talks about the details of the incident, working through it to ensure it does not affect them in the long run. They have follow-up conversations and check-ups with the mental health professional later on, as well. Cliff did not receive a critical stress debriefing, which could have mitigated some of his difficulties.

CHAPTER 18

PEOPLE ARE DEAD, AND I CAN'T DO ANYTHING ABOUT IT

THE BAUMAN FAMILY GREW UP IN rural Missouri. Cliff is the fourth of five children. All the siblings had a fun childhood. The family did not have a lot of money, but neither were they impoverished. There were times when they had a lot and times when they had little but each other. The family did a lot together, living in the country, moving around frequently. Cliff's father, Delbert Bauman, Sr., fished, hunted, and trapped all kinds of animals, including coyote, muskrat, and possum. He also worked the family garden through the year. He provided well for his family—they always had plenty of food to carry them through the Missouri winters. Cliff states that living simply makes you really appreciate the small things in life. His grandfather told him that the day he was born (after a long delivery), Cliff looked up with his big blue eyes, took a big yawn and fell asleep. From that moment he was happy and content.

The Bauman family. Photo credit: Clifford Bauman.

Cliff Bauman has been through the extremes. The lowest point of his life happened on 9/11 at the Pentagon. Cliff was there that day, searching through the rubble and debris looking for survivors for over eighteen hours; he found none. He climbed over human limbs, always to find a lifeless body but never a survivor. He searched this way for three days, without rest. Nothing could distract him from his goal.

After ending his search, Cliff returned to his home. He took off his uniform, boots, gloves, and hard hat, put them in a box, and put that box in the closet. The box remained there as a metaphor for his memories of the event, hidden. But they affected his life, no matter how much he denied it.

On the one-year anniversary of 9/11, Cliff was reading the *Washington Post* newspaper and saw the headline "One Year Later." His mind, having avoided the memories for the last twelve months, was no longer able to keep the box closed. In one article, a 10-year-old son had written a letter to his mother who had died at the Pentagon. Cliff saw her photo in the newspaper, and it was familiar. He had crawled over her body in the search and found her perfectly-intact wallet. The woman's name was Norma Khan. She had sat in seat C21 on American Airlines Flight 77.[64]

Cliff's brother, Dell, knew that Cliff had responded to the Pentagon on 9/11, and he got on a plane as soon as people were allowed to fly (all commercial flights had been suspended after the attacks). He knew that it was an unsettling event for Cliff, and none of the other siblings could make it to visit their brother, so he did. Cliff took Dell to the Pentagon and showed him what had happened and told him the story of what he had done in response. Cliff told his brother about seeing people that were sitting at their desk, and looked perfectly normal, like they were busy working—but they were dead. He told him that it was tough, and nothing can really prepare a person to see that. He showed Dell the boots and the uniform he had worn that day. They went to the overlook and saw the damage—basically a hole in the building. It was a mess. Dell wondered how the military was going to care for his brother, as Cliff was obviously in shock. Dell knew that Cliff's time on the scene had affected him in some way.

On December 22, 2002, Cliff was sleeping at Dell's house in Kansas City, Missouri. The guilt over not having saved anyone and a feeling of burdensomeness over making everyone in his life feel stress because of him became too much to handle. Life was not fun anymore. He felt that there was nothing left for him except guilt, despair, and being a burden to others. He decided that suicide was the answer to everything going on in his mind and to his relationships. He believed that ending his time on earth would finally bring silence to the nightmares and memories of the horrific images of 9/11. He wrote a suicide note on a paper towel that read, "I love you all, but the pain of not finding anyone alive is more than I can bear anymore."

He took twenty-two Ambien sleeping pills and laid down, planning on not waking up ever again. In his brother Dell's house, he drifted off to what he hoped would be a very deep, eternal sleep.

Dell was finishing his shift at work that night when something bizarre happened. He was working part-time at a different hospital and was attending an orientation to work in a unit he had never worked with before when he received a call at the desk where he was sitting. Dell normally worked in oncology, but that day he was in orthopedics. He did not know previously that he would be in that unit. The person on the other end of the line was his brother, Cliff. He still gets goose bumps to this day when he thinks of it. Dell has no explanation as to how Cliff found his number, or even knew where he would be that day.

"I don't know what to do. People are dead and I can't do anything about it. I've taken some pills, and I just can't do this."

Dell immediately dashed out toward his home. After the twenty-minute drive, Dell arrived to find his brother incoherent, but alive. He brought Cliff and the bottle of pills to Truman Medical Center, the only hospital in the downtown area of Kansas City, Missouri.

Downtown area hospitals in major cities have seen it all. Suicide attempts are a daily occurrence, and having worked in the emergency room, Dell knew what would happen to his brother when he brought him in. The staff got to work on Cliff right away.

To get the toxic drugs out of his system, they made him drink charcoal. As the charcoal started working, he became more alert.

As soon as Cliff became awake and alert, the first person he looked at was Dell. He stared at him and asked, "Are you God?"

Dell answered, "No, I am your brother."

The crazy mental fog in Cliff's mind, which happens to people when they come out of a deep reverie was pretty comical—that, combined with the fact that Cliff was alive and would heal, made for an emotional moment.

Dell knew that it was time for Cliff to seek help. He was also upset because he had not seen anything wrong with his brother prior to that attempt. His mind was full of thoughts and questions. Was he too close to the situation? Not close enough? Did he not ask the right questions? Why had Cliff not told him about his struggles? The family coped with tough situations by joking around, and Cliff used dark humor every now and then, but nothing that had triggered Dell's concern.

Cliff's suicide attempt has always bothered Dell because he believes that if he had known beforehand he would have been able to help Cliff and prevent any possibility of a suicide attempt. It is still inconceivable to Dell that pure chance or a miracle alone saved his brother's life.

When the brain fog dissolved, Cliff realized that he could not conquer the PTSD, survivor's guilt, depression, and alcoholism by himself, and that he really needed help. Recovering in the hospital is where Cliff learned that counseling was the answer for changing his life and finding a reason to live. Throughout his three-day stay in the Truman Medical Center mental health unit, he learned about therapy. Cliff realized that if he would take counseling seriously, it could save his life. After leaving the hospital, he started going to counseling again—he had received some therapy soon after 9/11, but his only goal then had been to get cleared for work. This time he did not cover everything up—he decided to tell his story and open up in order to gain insight and embrace living instead of dying.

Regulations on non-voluntary commitment vary by state, and in Missouri officials can commit a person to a psychiatric facility without their permission if they are a risk to themselves or others, due to a mental disorder. Cliff was a risk to himself and was committed to ninety-six hours of inpatient care. Cliff called Dell constantly, trying to get him to sign him out of the facility. It was aggravating to Dell, but he did not sign him out because he knew that it was important for Cliff to remain there for the duration. Finally, Cliff's older sister Tammie visited and signed him out. Dell was not happy about that. However, they stayed with Dell and by the time Cliff left, Dell was confident that he would take care of himself and address the issues that had led to his suicide attempt. Cliff was on the path of actively seeking help now, not just passively attending therapy sessions. He was ready to give his all to find healing by opening up to his therapists.

CHAPTER 19

OPERATE WITHIN THE REGULATIONS AND LAWS, AND DO YOUR BEST

DELL SHARES A BELIEF WITH MANY others that taking care of America means taking care of the people protecting it, whether that means supporting their mental health or physical health. "We need to make sure that happens. You should not be ostracized for seeking help, as service members often are in the military." Dell has a lot of strong opinions, but this one is driven by a deep concern that he may someday miss other signals from Cliff or others. He worries about Cliff relapsing, as often happens with survivors of suicide attempts.

Suicide intent has many different causes, and friends and family members do not always have all the facts. Dell has felt stress over not being able to stop Cliff's attempt. Dell had the fortune to get the call and make it back in time to bring Cliff to the hospital. A wrong number called, not hearing the telephone ring, or any other effect of chance could have prevented Dell from being able to save his brother's life. He would have had to deal with the fact that he did not have all the facts, and that his brother may have been reaching out in some way that Dell did not notice. He has since concluded that if there is nothing you can do to change the outcome, there is no reason to beat yourself up over not being there to help—if it was even possible. He resolved years ago that he would not beat himself up over Cliff's suicide attempt.

When someone goes into the emergency room for a suicide attempt, or for having the thought and a plan but not having attempted suicide yet, they undergo a mental health evaluation to get a closer look at what is going on. If family and friends are available, they may make a statement about what they have seen to help the doctor make an assessment. Getting another person committed against their will is a longer process. In the end, our choices over life and death belong to ourselves, and all a hospital or other civil or governmental entity can do is to buy a little time to help the person think about the impacts of their choice and find their reason to live.

Throughout his long career, Dell has seen the same patients progress through the years. His hospital takes care of indigent people and sees a lot of mental health issues, drug abuse, and suicidal behaviors at their hospital. However, they can only assess them during their hospital visits. Continuity of care is difficult because their visits are generally not very frequent. Once they are gone, they are on their own. Many times the patient completes suicide just after being released from the hospital. It can be a difficult conclusion to reach that involuntarily committing a person against their will can provide safety for a short time, but at the end of the day, everyone has their own life and makes their own choices. All hospital staff can do is to operate within the regulations and laws and do their best.

People who attempt suicide have different stories and reasons for their intent, all based on individual circumstances. Many are relationship-related, but not all. Hospital staff sees the whole gamut of reasons, from deep depression, to changes in life's outlook, to debilitating drug addiction. Sometimes overdoses may have been suicide attempts staged as an accidental overdose, and they investigate what led to the overdose to determine what type of help a person needs. Helping the patient find a reason and plan to live through the situation often takes more than the initial seventy-two hour involuntary commitment.

To require an involuntary commitment for more than seventy-two hours there must be a case review; facts are gathered and documented. The hospital staff brings the supporting documents and information before a judge in a formal courthouse hearing. The patient does not always go to the hearing, but they are invited. Patients go before the judge, but they are alone in their defense, with no advocate for their release if they are fighting involuntary commitment. In many cases, they have burned all their bridges. Patients with no family or friends are more likely to be committed for an extended time by judges.

Truman Medical Center has two hundred forty-nine beds throughout the hospital, including the emergency room, mental health department, labor and delivery, intensive care unit, and many outpatient clinics. The mental health facility takes up fifty of those beds. Having twenty percent of all a hospital's beds dedicated to mental health shows how much overlap there is between injuries and behavioral health. Very often there is a mental health component to physical injury and illness. Experienced medical providers report that the majority of hospital inpatients have a diagnosable behavioral health disorder. Such a high percentage of total beds being dedicated to the mental health unit supports that case.

Dell is the communication hub between units in his hospital, so he has knowledge of what is going on anywhere in the hospital at any given point. Every day people that attempt suicide or are seriously considering suicide come into the hospital. Medical providers evaluate patients that have self-inflicted cuts on their body, self-inflicted gunshot wounds, or that have accidentally or purposefully overdosed on pills and are seeking medical help. They join the patients with cuts inflicted from others during fights, persons with gunshot wounds inflicted by others, gang-related crime victims, and victims of other forms of violence. Throughout a shift, hospital staff sees it all. The first step providers take is to physically stabilize patients, then they address the mental health issues. These *always* play a role in self-harm cases. If there is a friend or family member with them, it makes it easier to assess the case—how many pills they have taken, how they got the wound, and exactly what the story is.

Inner city hospitals see repeat visitors often and get to know peoples' histories. The frequent customers are released and come back, again and again. Some people attempt suicide over and over again. For some, they seem to not be fully committed at the time; they know their limits and do not take it too far. Others may be doing it because they are homeless and need a place to stay, a meal, or just to get through the night. No matter the intent of the suicide attempt, safety issues result. For example, a patient may have an obstructed airway from throwing up what is in their system. When they are not awake or do not have the current cognitive capability to switch positions to remain breathing, they can vomit or otherwise experience an obstructed airway, even if they were not fully committed to dying from their self-harm action. Some drugs can depress your respiratory system and stop your breathing. There are drug interactions as well, which could be deadly. Alcohol and sleeping pills are a bad mix because they depress the central and autonomic nervous systems, which control bodily functions such as heart rate and breathing. When the nervous system runs without chemical interference, if a person holds their breath, their system knows they need to eventually take a breath. A person with a mixture of sleeping pills and alcohol in their system can lose the connection of their autonomic nervous system responses and die. Dell has seen that happen. Doctors need to know what a patient has taken to know the interactions they have to watch out for. Patients with suicide attempts require attention to medication and drug usage while being treated. Responding to these patients can be a complex situation.

Hospitals administer charcoal when they are treating a patient who has overdosed on medication or drugs. Activated charcoal absorbs medications and cleans out your system. Hospital staff can administer charcoal either in a drinkable form or through a tube they place into the nasal cavity. A nurse asked Dell how they should administer the charcoal to his brother to absorb the sleeping pills. Although the nasal option would be gentler and stop Cliff from tasting the charcoal, Dell believed that Cliff needed to remember that he did this to himself. He wanted Cliff to have a somewhat noxious experience. Remembering that there was charcoal involved in treating him would reinforce the negative aspects of the situation. He made sure Cliff received the drinkable form. After ingesting charcoal and counteracting the sleeping pills, Cliff was medically cleared and went to the mental health clinic.

Dell does not personally need help finding a reason to live as he does his best to help others find theirs. He has a strong will to live. He loves his family, especially his nieces and nephews. His loved ones give him a reason to live. In suicide prevention, we often see that family is the reason to live for someone. In suicide interventions, people often become interested in life when they consider how their suicide will affect their family members. However, family is not always enough for someone to put off suicide during the most stressful times in their lives. Others have different reasons to live—not always based on other people. Reasons to live can be as simple as a hope that something might change, and the person can find that reason and drive for life again with help.[65]

People naturally want to live, but too many do not see a way through all their problems. If they have a reason to live, they can find a way to live. Helping them find and focus on their reason, and then helping them take steps to get help will make their road to life fathomable. Sometimes it might be someone's job, especially if your job is fulfilling, or it may be helping others, like Dell does (that is another one of his reasons for living). Sometimes just searching for a reason to live or wanting to have a reason to live will be enough to get you up every morning to try again. When the drive to keep trying or keep looking for a reason gets weaker, the hold on life gets weaker. A medical provider, counselor, friend, family member, or acquaintance can help you find that life force again. No matter what system someone suffering from suicidal intentions falls into, the plan is always to treat them within the laws, doing everything possible to help them strengthen their life force, and then release them back into society as master of their future—a future now reinforced with a strong will to live.

CHAPTER 20

HOW MUCH WE CAN ACCOMPLISH IF OUR BRAIN WORKS FOR US, INSTEAD OF AGAINST US!

THINGS GOT BETTER FOR CLIFF AFTER he embraced counseling. He has had numerous counselors, and knows that if you don't trust them, nothing will change. Finding the right therapist, then, is extremely important in seeking help. If you are not comfortable talking with a counselor, you will not progress on your journey toward mental health. Many military service members believe that it is impossible to change therapists if there is no improvement, but Cliff knows that the therapist-patient relationship is crucial to effective treatment, and you must work in the system to find the right one.

Although it is hard to talk about personal, intense thoughts, it is important to do so. If it is in your mind, it is important enough to talk about. If it bothers you, you can work through it with the help of a trained professional counselor. Each counselor does things differently, even though they all train on a variety of empirically validated methods. Psychotherapy and counseling are where the art meets the science. Counselors and therapists use their verbal abilities to help their clients find better understanding of their thoughts and behaviors and to live the best life possible.

Some therapists have a goal for each session. Some try to instill lessons in each session through logotherapy or other techniques covered earlier. Some therapists just want to talk about what things are bothering you at the time or about how things are going. Therapists have different techniques to help with PTSD. A good therapist knows how to work with the specific client, according to what works best for them personally, and tailors the treatment to the client. What works for one does not necessarily work for another person, and no matter how state-of-the-art the therapist's technique is, there will always be a human component to therapy that must be met foremost. A therapist can miss the connection needed for symptom improvement if they are thinking too scientifically rather than trying to meet the client in their personal mental battle zone.

To change patients' decision-making habits to get them to think and act in a healthier way, counselors can use Cognitive Behavioral Therapy (CBT). How much we can accomplish if our brain works for us, instead of against us! That is what therapists aim to do with CBT. Counselors guide patients' minds through a journey into their own thought and behavior patterns and learn tools for identifying thinking traps and distortions that affect their ability to think clearly and make effective choices. CBT is a highly structured therapy program that can help individuals, as well as groups, with such issues as PTSD, phobias, depression, anxiety, eating disorders, and insomnia, among many other problems a first responder—or anyone else, for that matter—may experience.

CBT is a therapy that declares that mental health problems are very often founded in the client's unhealthy ways of thinking about certain situations. In previous situations, people learned the wrong lesson from their experience. These detrimental beliefs planted the seeds for good-for-nothing behavior. In the same way debriefing after a mission can lead to helpful lessons learned and a change in the way a person or group is prepared to respond to a future similar event, CBT can help a client grasp and incorporate healthy and beneficial ways of preparing for similar situations, adapt a more favorable and constructive behavior pattern, and cope better with past events. Developing practical and effective coping skills is a goal highly valued in the behavioral health field—as well as in education, business, law enforcement, and the military.

The United States Army has invested in numerous high-priced programs to improve resilience at both the individual and group level through expansive behavioral health resources, religious programs, and a CBT-based program called Master Resilience

Training (MRT), coordinated between the US Army and the University of Pennsylvania's Positive Psychology Center. The MRT program is based on CBT for groups of people instead of individuals. MRT coaches complete rigorous training to become group-level CBT coaches for their unit. MRT was initially developed for the grade-school setting but transfers over to the military population if it is employed in a coaching format, rather than a didactic, PowerPoint-based lesson format. MRT has helped countless people understand their own thinking and finally take control of their minds.[66]

All the current resilience programs and resources did not exist when Cliff attempted suicide in 2002. However, through his experience with the programs, he believes that they would have helped him and that he would not have attempted suicide if he had the skills that he has since gained from the MRT program and other military resources. In the years since 9/11, Cliff has realized that the memories and some of the symptoms of PTSD might never go away, but you can make your life better by learning coping skills to deal with the triggers that may show up. Social support is also an important part of being strong while going through PTSD or any other illness or disorder. The skills gained from MRT and learned from therapists have helped Cliff both personally and professionally.

CHAPTER 21

WHOA, WHOA, WHOA, TIMEOUT— WHO IS THAT?

IF CLIFF'S LIFE HAD ENDED THAT day, he would never have had the chance to marry his wife, Krystal, raise his two sons, or meet all the people he has encountered at speaking events.

One of the most important and consequential positions for army operations success is the Unit Movement Officer (UMO). The UMO plans and coordinates all logistics for moving people, supplies, and gear. Without a UMO, nothing happens. Cliff was deployed in Iraq in 2007 as a UMO, in charge of shuttling air crews when they needed to fly from one base to another. One of his duties involved flying other service members back and forth from Iraq to Camp Arifjan in Kuwait. Cliff would drop crews off and then stay for a day or two. He was happy with that task because Camp Arifjan was a nicer base than the main base he was stationed at in Kuwait—Camp Beuhring. During one of their trips, his boss, an Army major, saw one of his friends from college who was also stationed at Camp Afrijan. They talked a little bit and decided to meet up later, and the group would have lunch together at the dining facility. That lunch meeting would change Cliff's life forever—in a good way.

The group sat in the chow hall in Kuwait, and the major and his college friend were talking, as they had not seen each other since college, about twenty years ago. The major's friend normally ate lunch with a nurse named Krystal Turner. Krystal walked up to the table to tell her friend that she was there but was going to sit at another table. Now, this seemed like a normal exchange for her and Krystal, but for Cliff, when Krystal walked up to the table, it felt like the whole dining facility became quiet, and it seemed like she was walking through a tunnel as she came to talk with her friend.

At that time, Cliff was a newly promoted Chief Warrant Officer 3 (CW3) and was an unknown soldier to others stationed at the base. Krystal did not pay attention or notice him. She told her friend that she was at another table because she did not care too much for some other persons at the table, the story goes. She walked off and everyone resumed their conversations. Everyone except for Cliff.

"Who, whoa, whoa, timeout—who is that? I have to meet her!" said Cliff.

The major's friend kept pestering Krystal to meet Cliff for a couple of weeks until she finally gave in. The two were friends for a while before they started seeing each other romantically. Things eventually took off and they have been together since late 2007.

After the deployment, Krystal returned to Chicago and Cliff returned to Virginia. Their relationship relied on phone calls for the most part, until they had a quiet summer elopement on June 4, 2009. Nobody in either of their families was aware of their secret marriage. A little over a year later, on October 23, 2010, the couple had what they would call a "real" wedding in Krystal's home state of Massachusetts at a countryside bed and breakfast with a separate venue for events. Cliff's family flew in, and it was a perfect fall day. However, after the wedding, the families flew home, and Krystal once again returned to Chicago while Cliff returned to Virginia. They were geographically separated by their lives as military professionals, as often happens.

Krystal is from the Caribbean island of Trinidad. When the couple finally got to take a long-awaited honeymoon, that is where they went. They spent thirty days there enjoying island activities. They saw leatherback sea turtles—the largest of all living turtles—come up on the beach and lay eggs. When they came to the beach, usually in the middle of the night, the hotel would call the guests up to come see the incredible sight. It was pitch black on the beach, with no moon, and guests would use a red-beamed flashlight to see the turtles so as not to bother, blind, or scare the creatures. On one such occasion, Cliff and Krystal saw a turtle far down on the far side of the beach, and they started walking toward it in the pitch black. The couple stumbled on another one, this one about six feet long! This jumbo sea turtle did not have a registration tag on its body, meaning it was not registered with the island. A scientist tracking the turtles heard about their find and came over to meet up with them. Finders of unregistered turtles are given the great privilege of naming the animal. Another couple, with their young son, also came over to see the new, giant turtle, and Cliff gave the naming privilege to the boy, which thrilled him. The turtle, now named after the kid, spent some time on the beach laying her eggs and making some fake nests as well, and then headed back into the ocean.

After their honeymoon, Cliff and Krystal had to continue living apart, but they put their paperwork in to request to be stationed in the same region the next time they were up for their next permanent change of station. It would be a little tricky, with Krystal being an active duty sailor and Cliff an active duty soldier serving in the national guard. Their choices for locations were limited, as it required harmonizing two branches (navy and army), two components (active duty and national guard), units specializing in their career fields (medical and aviation) with vacancies for their ranks, and bases positioned in close proximity to each other. It would likely be in the DC area.

After four years together spiritually as husband and wife, but separated geographically, the couple finally moved in together when Krystal got stationed at Portsmouth, Virginia, just 20 miles south of Cliff's station in Fort Monroe, Virginia. The couple stayed there through 2014, about the time Krystal became pregnant with their son, Llyod. After Portsmouth, Virginia, in April 2014, Krystal was stationed at Fort Belvoir, Virginia, and they were again separated until October of that year when they moved to Woodbridge, Virginia, as Cliff was stationed at the NGB headquarters in Northern Virginia. They now both had manageable commutes and could live together as a military family. Dual-military families such as the Baumans have support from military resources such as childcare and housing, as well as morale, welfare, and recreation programs. They have a caregiver that comes to watch the children when they are out of town for work, and generally have things set up in a satisfactory manner for their lifestyle.

Krystal and Cliff, taken a week after they met. Photo credit: Clifford Bauman.

Although they may have to go through another military separation if either of them gets relocated before retiring, they understand the needs of the military for their officer specialties sometimes take precedence over keeping military families together. But they also know that separations are temporary. The military does the best they can to keep families co-located. With a cross-branch family such as the Baumans—one being in the army and one in the navy—and with both of them going further up in rank and requiring specific key and developmental assignments, they may have to separate again before their service is up and they can enjoy a well-earned retirement. Being an active-duty military officer requires a service member to advance through progressive key and developmental position assignments. Keeping in contact in the current day and age is easy, though, thankfully. They are both busy in their jobs and think differently than most of their civilian counterparts, who can progress through their career without making moves to a different location every few years. For their counterparts, career growth can take place in the same state, city, or even building. For military officers, the higher-level positions a career officer will need to grow are not always available at the same base, or even in the same state. The needs of the army would then take precedence, and an officer would relocate to where they are assigned. This covers both in-state assignments and overseas deployments—as in the one where Cliff and Krystal met.

CHAPTER 22

I SAW A SET OF ANGEL
WINGS BEHIND YOU

GOING BACK TO THE EARLY 1600S, Fort Monroe, Virginia, holds an important place in United States history. Located on the Chesapeake Bay in Hampton, Virginia, at the southern tip of the Virginia Peninsula, Fort Monroe is about thirty miles southeast of the first English Colony in the United States: Jamestown, Virginia. It was the largest stone fort ever built and the site where Jefferson Davis, the former Confederate president, was imprisoned for two years after the Civil War. The fort was decommissioned under the 2005 base realignment and closure (BRAC) process proposal of May 13, 2005—which was nicknamed "BRAC Friday." After discussions and a failed House of Representatives joint resolution, the Secretary of Defense was forced to close and realign many military bases by September 15, 2011. Fort Monroe was closed on September 11, 2011 and is now a national monument.[67]

Cliff lived with his family at Fort Monroe before it was

decommissioned in 2011. On October 3, 2009, his 5-year-old son, Clifford Bauman, Jr., called "Junior" by his family and friends, wanted to drift fish for flounder and red drum out in front of their house, about five miles offshore in the Chesapeake Bay. The Chesapeake Bay exists in its current form and location due to the impact from a meteor or comet roughly thirty-five million years ago.[68] Cliff did not particularly care to drift fish that day, as he had never really caught many fish out there, but of course he would do it to oblige his son.

Cliff took his best friend, Rick Marquis, and Junior on his new boat, the *Krystal Marie* (named after his wife). They motored around Fort Monroe, heading about five miles northeast to start drift fishing. It was a calm day at sea with temperatures in the mid-sixties and winds under ten miles an hour from the southwest. The crew wore shorts and t-shirts. By all standards, it was a normal October day.

The *Krystal Marie* was a white and light blue Seahunt Victory 225 LE—a 22½-foot boat. The group arrived at a good location for drift fishing, shut down the engine, and floated with the current. There were a lot of ships going in and out of the port while Cliff, Rick, and Junior drift fished from the deck of the *Krystal Marie*. Cliff and his crew were proficient swimmers and had life jackets within reach. The waves in that spot were about one to three feet high. A barge navigated the channel further out from them in deeper water.

The three were enjoying the day, but Cliff was eyeing a small, 17-foot vessel in the path of a tugboat that was pushing a two-story barge—about 140 feet long—right toward the little boat.

Cliff said to Rick, "This does not look good! That small vessel is not going to move, and the barge is likely to hit it. We better prepare for the worst."

Rick agreed, and the group brought in their fishing lines, grabbed the Coast Guard bag from the cuddy cabin on the boat's deck, and started motoring toward the area, preparing themselves to help if what seemed likely to happen did, in fact, happen.

Cliff and his crew reached the scene just as the barge hit the small vessel for the first time. The weight of the barge pushed the small boat away from it and the small boat rocked back towards the barge. One of the sailors in the small boat stood up and yelled at the large boat, "Hey, hey, hey, wait, wait, wait, wait, hey!" The large boat hit the small boat again, this time capsizing it, sending it under the large boat. The small boat was completely under water for a moment, and then popped up on the other side of the barge. The sailors on the small boat were in grave danger. Cliff, Rick, and Junior were the only ones in the vicinity, as it was early in the morning and not many boats were braving the wavy conditions.

As the small vessel reappeared after being submerged in the 10-12-foot-deep water, Cliff maneuvered the *Krystal Marie* closer to the scene. Using the on-board marine radio and GPS, Cliff and his crew called in exact locations to authorities—direct north of the *Krystal Marie*, north-northwest, five miles from the peninsula where he lived. Three of the sailors were holding onto the capsized vessel, and another sailor was swimming nearby. The swimmer's movements stopped, no longer propelling himself through arm and leg strokes. He was afloat, facedown, and at that time Cliff made the conscious decision to take action.

In a split-second decision, Cliff took off his shirt, donned a life vest and, carrying three more life vests, dove into the 60-degree water, which was now volatile due to gas and debris from the collision. Five-year-old Junior immediately reacted, crying for his father to get back into the boat. Cliff swam to the first sailor, 55-year-old Lieutenant (LT) James Newsome from Wake, North Carolina. Newsome, a county deputy, was about 20 feet away from the *Krystal Marie*. He was not breathing. Cliff flipped him over and began administering cardiopulmonary resuscitation (CPR).

CPR works by pumping the heart to circulate blood throughout the body, particularly to the brain, to deliver essential oxygen. Administering CPR involves quickly shifting between forceful and quick chest compressions at about 100-120 pumps per minute and breathing two bursts of oxygen to the lungs after each set of thirty compressions. Although it can be very helpful in keeping oxygenated blood in the brain while waiting for more effective life-resuscitative treatment, such as a defibrillator, it is much less effective than shown in the movies. Bringing someone back to life with CPR alone happens only in a small percent of cases. It is worth the effort, though, as it can be successful and gives the person a shot at life.

Effective CPR while in the water is virtually impossible.

However, Cliff attempted to do CPR right there. Every time Cliff pushed on LT Newsome's chest, he went back under water. He was foaming at the mouth, which made CPR even more difficult. Cliff needed to move the sailor to a steady, fixed area to continue the CPR procedure.

As Cliff was starting to move the first sailor to a more solid, firm location, another vessel showed up. By chance, the new vessel was manned by one of Cliff's friends, Sergeant Major (SGM) Timothy Bushee, and his father. The group tried to get LT Newsome onto SGM Bushee's 22-foot Bayliner Trophy boat, but he was just too heavy, and the boat's shape made it even more difficult. Cliff put the life vest on him so he would not sink, and then attempted further to get him on the boat. With much physical force, he succeeded. The group then rushed him to the shore. SGM Bushee, who was trained in combat lifesaver—a required army first aid course—continued CPR during the trip to the shore and once they arrived, but without success. James Newsome passed away from an apparent heart attack at the age of fifty-five, but not alone, and not without substantial effort made to try to save his life by a group of willing first responders.

Now that Newsome was out of the water, Cliff went to work to assist the other three sailors—Kenneth Evans, 57; Tilghman Hall, 70; and William Thompson, 73, all from Raleigh, North Carolina. It was apparent to Cliff that none of the sailors could swim, as they were struggling to stay afloat on the water. Cliff swam back to the capsized vessel carrying three life vests. He pulled himself up on top of the vessel and proceeded to put life vests on each of the three sailors as they clung to the boat. All the sailors were large men. The largest of them was, Cliff estimated, about 300 pounds. As he panicked during the rescue, Cliff had to explain to him that since he had a life vest on, he was not going to sink. The situation was intense, and Cliff added that if he did not calm down, he would leave him in the water.

Junior was beside himself in the *Krystal Marie*, anxiously watching his father try to help three resistant sailors reach safety. The group decided that the best way to get the large man into Cliff's boat was to back it up to the capsized vessel and use physical force to maneuver the men up the ladder. Fitness and strength training have always been a part of Cliff's life, and it paid off for him that day!

Rick was a soldier, a sergeant major—the highest enlisted rank attainable. He was a little older than Cliff, had brown hair and the same athletic build as Cliff, and enjoyed the same water sports and fishing as his friend. He was also proficient at multitasking. Rick was in contact with the Coast Guard and other authorities, while at the same time managing to keep the boat the correct distance to avoid letting the current push the *Krystal Marie* into the capsized vessel. He backed the boat up to the damaged craft, and Cliff rested his back against it, with the ladder down. Cliff then set each sailor on his lap and then he and Rick would push and pull each of the men to the boat. They started with the biggest guy, because he logically would be the hardest to bring up and would require the most physical strength. Cliff put his back to the vessel and he and Rick pushed and pulled about seven or eight times until the man was up in the boat. This was no easy feat, even in calm waters, let alone the choppy waves. The process took about fifteen minutes for the first man. The whole time, Cliff was being banged against the boat by three-foot swells.

After rescuing the largest sailor, Cliff swam back for the next one. He was a bit younger than his companion and a lot lighter. It was not as difficult to get him into the boat as it had been for the first round. After some work, he pretty much crawled into the boat by himself. The third man was tangled up, tied to the capsized vessel with various fishing gear and items. Cliff cut him free with pocketknife and thanked God that the vessel had not sunk, dragging the sailor down with it. The man was now untangled; however, his leg was stiff as a board, and he was paralyzed by his fear of drowning. At that moment though, Cliff had a rush of adrenaline, and as you often hear in stories of people performing actions that are physically beyond their capabilities, Cliff succeeded in throwing the man from the water, over the engine, and into the *Krystal Marie*.

This entire rescue took about 45 minutes, and the water was cold, about 60°F. Cliff was becoming hypothermic. Rick pulled Cliff up from the water and into the boat. Just as that happened, the captain of the tugboat that started the incident by hitting the smaller boat, pulled his boat and the barge around, making it to the accident scene.

The captain was defensive. "What is going on? What happened? I did not hit anything!"

Cliff became very short with the man, telling him "I don't have time to talk with you. I have to take the injured sailors to the marina." He resumed assessing the three sailors in the boat regarding their health and condition, as well as calming down Junior. Now, Cliff is a good soldier, able to juggle many priorities at once, and remained calm while the captain is swearing that he didn't hit a boat. As he was going on about this, Cliff reiterated to him that he was getting in the way and should remove himself from the situation for the time being. Then Cliff and his crew and the sailors motored down to Fort Monroe.

The crew arrived at the Old Point Comfort Marina on Fort Monroe. They motored past the hundreds of boats secured to the floating docks, the marina maintenance facilities and fuel pumps, and the store and seafood restaurant to meet the marine patrol that was anticipating their arrival. The marine patrol assisted in unloading the sailors. Afterward, Cliff, Rick, Junior, and SGM Bushee and his father sat down with the military police, filling out forms and going over the incident with them.

The big guy who had been rescued looked at Cliff, came up to him, and gave him a big hug. With tears in his eyes, he stated: "You know, I thought I was gonna die. I thought I was a goner. The moment you jumped into the boat, I saw a set of angel wings behind you. At that moment, I knew I was gonna live." That struck a chord with Cliff, and he still gets a little choked up when he talks about hearing the man say that to him.

The other two sailors heard the encounter and told Cliff and the marine patrol that they agree with the statement. They agreed he had angel wings that day. The marine patrol was also appreciative of Cliff and his crew's hard work in saving the men that day. They stated that it was very lucky that Cliff, Rick, and Junior were around in the *Krystal Marie*, or the patrol would have probably gotten word of the capsized vessel days later and would probably never have found the gentlemen.[69]

CHAPTER 23

I CAN'T BELIEVE SOMEBODY WOULD DO THAT FOR ANOTHER PERSON OUT OF KINDNESS

THE CRUSHING IMPACTS ON CLIFF'S BODY from slamming against the boat during the rescue took its toll on his back. Cliff states that it looked like someone had taken a baseball bat to his back, as it was beat up, scratched, and heavily bruised. Cliff went to sick call on the Fort Monroe base and received treatment for a bruised back and legs, scratches, cuts, and abrasions. They gave him bandages, dressings, and first aid treatment. The *Krystal Marie* was just as beat up as he was.

Initially, local newspapers gave credit to the Coast Guard and local emergency rescue teams for the rescues, which obviously irritated the *real* rescuers—Cliff and his partners. Many boats passed without offering help, and the Coast Guard was not involved until after all sailors were at the marina. Cliff attempted to set the record straight in a couple of newspaper interviews, explaining that the Coast Guard was not actually there or involved during the 45-minute rescue. They trained in the vicinity and were in the area and could have helped, but they were not active in the rescue. That they took credit in an earlier newscast really hurt Cliff because he felt guilt over losing LT Newsome, whereas if the Coast Guard had shown up when Cliff's team radioed in the exact location of the accident, the man's life might have been saved.

The *Krystal Marie* sustained quite a bit of damage during the rescue from debris such as fishing gear, boat pieces, and gas and oil floating around, banging the hull of the light blue and white fishing boat. The boat was three months old, as Cliff had bought it brand new in July that year, and the incident happened in October. It was damaged, but a good boat. Cliff took the boat out of the water with his trailer and scheduled an appointment to have it repaired at Norfolk Marine, where he had bought it. When Cliff dropped off the boat, the service manager started ribbing him, giving him a hard time because the boat was new, and there it was, already damaged. He changed his attitude when Cliff told him the story of how the boat incurred the damage.

Norfolk Marine was founded by Garland L. Kight, Sr., in 1946. His son, Mr. Garland Kight, Jr., came to work there full-time in 1973. Garland Kight, Sr., passed the business to his son, Garland Kight, Jr., before passing away. Garland Kight, Jr., sold it to his son-in-law, who sold it late 2021.[70] The company took about two months to fix the boat. The service manager called Cliff one day and told him the boat was finished. He went right away to retrieve the *Krystal Marie*. She was completely repaired and once again in pristine shape. Cliff asked for the bill, but the service manager instead told him Norfolk Marine's owner, Mr. Garland Kight, Sr. wanted to talk with him about what happened. Cliff had told the story a few times to various people and thought the owner wanted to hear the story out of curiosity and then give him the bill. Cliff replied that he would be happy to talk to him.

Mr. Kight, Sr., was a big guy, tall with grey hair. He has a welcoming personality and ran a very professional business. Cliff went to see him in his office off to the side of the showroom. They had a casual conversation, and Cliff told Mr. Kight, Sr., the story of how the *Krystal Marie* became damaged. Mr. Kight, Sr., smiled at the end of the story and told Cliff, "You know, I'm a fisherman too, and I appreciate what you did. There was about $5,000 worth of damage to your boat, and we're gonna go ahead and fix your boat for free." To this day, Cliff is emotional when he thinks of Mr. Kight, Sr., and how somebody would do that for another person out of kindness. Of course, Mr. Kight, Sr., thought the same thing about Cliff.

Cliff learned that the man who passed away was a retired US Army soldier named James Newsome. As Cliff recovered from his own injuries, he dwelled on the fact that he could not save him. The group had traveled up from North Carolina to do some fishing and just did not understand the nautical rules of the road and that you must get out of the path of commercial vessels. The big sailor who told Cliff about his angel wings also told him that he thought the big vessel was just going to move out of their way, but it did not move out of the way. It was a tragedy that never should have happened. Once again, Cliff let something out of his control get to him. He needed insight from outside once again to gain perspective and find a way to move ahead.

A psychiatric nurse friend told Cliff, "You know, it is awfully easy for us to always think about the negative things in life, and we gravitate to that. We do that as a human species. But one thing you have to remember is that there are three gentlemen that went home that day that never would have seen their families again if you had not been there and done what you did. You did it to the best of your ability and did what you needed to do at that time, and there's nothing else you could have done." He was right, and Cliff understood. Sometimes we become tunnel-visioned and need someone from outside to give us insight. A good counselor or friend can change our life. This insight changed Cliff's trajectory.

With time, Cliff felt better about the entire incident. However, sometimes he is still bothered by the memory of October 3, 2009. People who suffer PTSD have triggers, and the dates of September 11 and October 3 are triggers for him. But Cliff has learned to take the negative, turn it into a positive, and just accept that there are some things you can control and some things you cannot control. Bad things still happen no matter what you do to intervene. Coping this way has saved Cliff. These insights have come from reflection, often guided by therapists and counselors.

CHAPTER 24

FOR HEROISM

THE SOLDIER'S MEDAL IS THE HIGHEST medal a soldier can be awarded when completing a heroic act not during conflict with an armed enemy. The medal requires the performance of a heroic act while placing oneself at risk. It is not based only on saving another person's life, but the soldier must have gone into harm's way in their action. The army first awarded the Soldier's Medal in 1927 to three soldiers for two separate heroic acts: rushing into a burning building that contained explosives and jumping into a lake to rescue a boy from drowning.[71] Since then, the Soldier's Medal has continued to be awarded to soldiers who put themselves in danger to save others. However, it is rarely awarded and requires approval at the highest levels.

Chief Bauman's actions on October 3, 2009, led to his second nomination for the Soldier's Medal. After 9/11, a leader at the NGB drafted awards packets to give Cliff and Jack Soldier's Medals, and Bob an Airman's Medal—which is the Air Force's equivalent of the Soldier's Medal. However, all three awards were downgraded to commendation medals because higher leadership decided that persons not inside the building during the attack were excluded from receiving any medals for valor. The decision was administrative and over-ran the nomination from a three-star general. However, Cliff's second nomination was approved for his bravery in October 2009.

On July 23, 2010, CW3 Clifford Bauman received the Soldier's Medal for his selfless actions in saving lives in the Chesapeake Bay. He was a member of the Virginia Army National Guard at the time of the actions but was serving full-time on active-duty orders with the US Army Training and Doctrine Command at Fort Eustis in Virginia. The ceremony was at the Morelli Auditorium at Joint Base Langley-Eustis in Newport News, Virginia. His citation for the medal reads:

The President of the United States of America, authorized by Act of Congress, 2 July 1926,

has awarded the SOLDIER'S MEDAL to

CHIEF WARRANT OFFICER THREE CLIFFORD W. BAUMAN UNITED STATES ARMY ACCESSIONS COMMAND

FOR HEROISM: on 3 October 2009, while responding to a boating accident. After witnessing a barge collide with a small boat in the Chesapeake Bay, Chief Warrant

Officer Three Bauman immediately began to radio for help as he piloted his craft towards the accident. Upon reaching the scene and realizing that the injured fishermen who had been thrown overboard from the collision were unable to swim, he acted with complete disregard for his own safety, grabbing several life vests and diving into the water. Swimming through water contaminated by an oil slick, he reached one fisherman and immediately began emergency CPR after finding him laying motionless and face down in the water. After bringing the unconscious man to another boat which had arrived to help, Chief Warrant Officer Three Bauman then swam to the sinking fishing boat where the other three fishermen were struggling to stay above water. Over the next forty minutes, he helped each fisherman in turn don a life vest and aided them as they swam to the safety of another boat. Chief Warrant Officer Three Bauman's tireless efforts, at great risk to his own life, undoubtedly saved the lives of the four[72] fishermen and serve as an example for all soldiers to follow. Chief Warrant Officer Three Bauman's selfless and heroic actions are in keeping with the finest traditions of military service and reflect great credit upon himself, the United States Army Accessions Command, and the United States Army.[73]

Cliff's wife, his father, and his friends, co-workers, and colleagues, as well as other soldiers attended the event. Lieutenant

General (LG) John E. Sterling, Jr., Deputy Commander for US Army Training Doctrine and Command, pinned the medal on Cliff. The four-star General, Martin Dempsey, would have awarded him the medal, but he was recovering from an illness, so his deputy filled in for him. LG Sterling remarked that it was his first time awarding the Soldier's Medal, and that it was a significant event for him. "The army has many awards for soldiers displaying valor during battle, but this is the highest medal for valor while not engaged in combat. We are proud of having you on our team, Mr. Bauman."

Cliff receiving his Soldier's Medal. Photo credit: Clifford Bauman.

Prior to the event LG Sterling spoke with Cliff's family and friends. He dismissed everyone but Cliff so he could talk with him in private. They discussed the event, and he stated that it was an honor for him to bestow the award and that he had not had the privilege to give the Soldier's Medal because it was so rare. He said, "Normally, I would be the last to walk into the room for such a ceremony, but I want you to have that honor because of the medal. I am going to get up after the ceremony and make some comments, and then I am going to give the microphone over to you to speak so you can say your closing comments. But one thing—I want to ensure that you leave the Coast Guard out of your statements!" The General knew Cliff, and he knew politics and all about public perceptions. Leaving behind the animosity over their taking credit for the event would be the best for everybody. Cliff responded, "Yes, Sir, I'll leave the Coast Guard out of my statements," which he observed on that day and in further interviews.

Cliff told the group, "There are ordinary folks like us who are often at the site of emergencies and disasters, and if soldiers find themselves in such situations or circumstances where they can safely offer assistance, we should do so."

Soldiers are trained for emergency events, which do not only happen in battle. The number of Soldier's Medals awarded since the award's approval for use in 1927 proves Cliff's statement that soldiers often find themselves in emergencies and are successful at using their training in these cases. Cliff continued, "Soldiers' training in making quick decisions based on the situation and resources available saves lives literally daily. Soldiers in the Army Reserve Command and in the Army National Guard often use their life-saving skills in their civilian careers as well. It can come natural for soldiers to step in during life-and-death situations."

CHAPTER 25

MAKING THE CONNECTION

SOLDIERS OFTEN SEE MENTAL HEALTH CARE as undesirable. In some bases, mental health clinics are far from the hospital or where soldiers live and work. It can seem inaccessible. Cliff was not in the slightest bit convinced that he really needed treatment for his PTSD. Although PTSD in the military and first responder populations is higher than it is in the general population, due to exposure to trauma, risk, and stress in the context of their job, service members and other first responders can be doubtful of the positive effect therapy can have on their lives and their careers. Therefore, although PTSD is a serious, treatable disorder, many service members do not seek help. They tend to attach more stigma to conceding the existence of a psychological problem than they do to seeking treatment for medical problems. That stigma prevents many soldiers, sailors, airmen, marines, coast guardsmen, and other first responders from seeking effective treatment and leaves them unable to deal with PTSD.

Soldiers have been concerned for decades over losing their security clearance, and possibly their military careers, if they were to admit to seeking help for a mental health issue. All service members have some level of a security clearance. They complete a form when they enlist or commission as an officer, and they complete periodic security clearance recertifications, depending on their level of clearance. Although the initial 1964 version of the "DD-398 - Statement of Personal History" form had no mental health questions, later versions inquired about mental health. The 1981 version asked, "Have you ever been a patient (whether or not formally committed) in any institution primarily devoted to the treatment of mental, emotional, psychological, or personality disorders?" The 1990 version went on to ask, "Have you ever been treated for a mental, emotional, psychological, or personality disorder/condition/problem?" and "Have you ever consulted or been counseled by any mental health professional?" The 1995 version finally made an attempt to destigmatize counseling in some circumstances with the question, "In the last 7 years, have you consulted with a mental health professional (psychiatrist, psychologist, counselor, etc.) or have you consulted with another health care provider about a mental health related condition?" followed by, "If you answered 'Yes,' provide an entry for each treatment to report, unless the consultation(s) involved only marital, family, or grief counseling, not related to violence by you."[74]

In 2008, the questionnaire went on to destigmatize seeking help for adjustment issues related to military service and included the statement, "Mental health counseling in and of itself is not a reason to revoke or deny a clearance." The electronic questionnaire asked, "In the last 7 years, have you consulted with a health care professional regarding an emotional or mental health condition or were you hospitalized for such a condition? Answer 'No' if the counseling was for any of the following reasons and was not court-ordered: 1) strictly marital, family, grief not related to violence by you; or 2) strictly related to adjustments from service in a military combat environment."

Still, the stigma endures, as service members are concerned over losing their security clearance or being put on a medical profile, which would affect their deployability and possible duties and promotions. Additionally, a concern remains that others might not have confidence in them, treatment could contaminate their medical records, or they would be treated in a different manner by their leaders if they sought mental health care. Further adding to this stigma is the assumption that seeking treatment is a sign of weakness. This is one case where assumptions can be incorrect—and deadly.

The truth is that seeking help can actually save your career. Moreover, treatment can enhance your career and your life in general. Modern military leaders see seeking help as a true sign of strength. Seeking treatment for mental health issues should no longer harm a service member's military career. Cliff Bauman is an agent of this message. His goal is to change the way the army thinks about PTSD and mental health support, in order to save lives.

The military is in a campaign to change the way its members view mental health support, thanks in small part to Cliff's work. Military leaders now promote help-seeking behavior. The security clearance questionnaire does not put military members' careers at risk when they seek help for PTSD or other "adjustments from service in a military combat environment."

Military commands routinely bring in mental health professionals to educate the troops in help-seeking behavior, especially for PTSD, depression, alcohol and substance use, and suicide ideation. After training sessions with mental health professionals, service members' frames of mind change, and they evaluate the effectiveness of PTSD treatment more highly. Mental health professionals show them how and where to seek PTSD treatment. They become more open to seeking help for PTSD if it is a problem for them.

The stigma around mental health is not just a military issue. Across all demographics, only a small percentage of people that have mental health issues actually seek treatment. Access to care is not the main issue—the hesitation is due to the stigma and incorrect information about mental health treatment. Soldiers need to know that their responses to traumatic stress are common to the point of being predictable and can be successfully treated. They would have support and their career will be improved rather than blemished or damaged in some way.

The good news is that help-seeking for mental health difficulties is on the rise. The campaign to destigmatize mental health must be working! However, the bad news is that over half of military members who report depression, PTSD, or other emotional and mental afflictions also report that they are not seeking treatment for these problems.[75] The reality is that those who have the most stigma and adversarial beliefs about help-seeking behavior are also the ones facing the most mental health difficulties. The more symptoms a person has, the less likely they are to take advantage of mental health treatment resources.[76] Issues such as depression, substance abuse, sleep disorders, PTSD, and relationship difficulties compound. Without dealing with these issues, life gets harder.

The science behind treating mental health issues is rapidly progressing. Traditional, controlled experiments and quasi-experiments can validate treatments with strong methodological rigor, reliability, and validity that allows them to call their results objective. The art and the science converge in clinical psychology. A new wave of psychologists, behavioral researchers, and policy professionals wants the thinking about mental health to evolve into being a normal part of holistic health.

Leaders' emphasis on seeking help, as well as training sessions from mental health providers, aim to reduce the stigma. They change the cultural climate and educate service members about treatment's success. Putting a face to stigma-reduction programs is another way to get people the help they need.[77] To prevent suicide, we need to recast the way people see mental health and transform their attitudes. We need to show actual serving members who have sought help and attained peace and success in the military. By telling personal stories, like Cliff's, and through their testimony of what was going on with them before, during, and after treatment, we can unmask the unseen warrior who sought help for PTSD and offer an alternate model that others who are suffering silently can follow.

The army has adopted this approach with numerous public service announcements and various messages from high-level officers and enlisted military leaders. Many leaders faced their own battles with PTSD and depression before making it to the highest levels of military service. Empathetic and effective leaders that make their struggles public reinforce that seeking help is not a sign of weakness, and it will not harm your career. Modeling mental health care as a customary reaction, instead of an admission of a shortcoming can free many people who are confining their suffering due to stigma. A new perspective and a new attitude can free you.

By showing a new way to be a soldier, sailor, airman, marine, or coast guardsman, leaders like 38th Chief of Staff of the Army, General (retired) Raymond T. Odierno;[78] former Director of Army Forces Command, Major General (retired) Mark A. Graham;[79] 14th Sergeant Major of the Army (retired) Raymond F. Chandler;[80] and other leaders, including Cliff Bauman, are shattering the assumption that the military will not support those facing PTSD and depression, that PTSD is not normal, that seeking help will ruin your career, and that treatment is not effective. By presenting accurate information regarding current policies and improving the overall command ethos and attitude, the armed forces leadership will ease the minds of its service members who are avoiding treatment as the need for it increases. This can lead to more effective and less stressed and anxious troops.

The army also teaches suicide prevention in standardized courses. Mental health and suicide prevention training are conducted at large and small events, often before, during, or after a deployment. Program managers and unit training personnel plan many different courses. Some are short sessions. Some are half-day courses. Some are a full day, two days, or even longer. There are different audiences for the different standardized courses. Some mostly cover how to identify behaviors and refer someone to professional help and do not go into much detail about the treatment options, effectiveness of treatment, or examples of what treatment can do for you. The longer courses are for service members of certain positions that regularly deal with suicide and persons at risk of suicide. Those personnel are called "gatekeepers."

Units who cannot attend in-person events with leaders who survived PTSD can show videos about suicide prevention, mental health treatment, and other subjects. The videos are not a stand-alone presentation though, as generally, trainers will deliver their material and use leaders' videos on help-seeking behavior, treatment, and successful careers, as substantiation to reinforce their message. The higher the level of a leader or presenter, the more successful a presentation can be at reducing the stigma around mental health treatment. Cliff's August 2012 YouTube video "Make the Connection—A harrowing personal journey after 9/11" has been used to support unit-level suicide prevention training thousands of times.

The predominant barriers stopping first responders and

service members from seeking PTSD treatment are that they are unwilling to accept that they have PTSD, that they feel a stigma over having PTSD, or that they are unaware of their PTSD symptoms. Service members might believe that PTSD treatment is not effective and that mental health professionals are not trustworthy. Other obstacles may be that they do not know how to get help or believe they would have a tough time scheduling and attending treatment for logistical reasons. These are myths and assumptions that military leaders, policy experts, and behavioral health scientists must work to address.

No matter how carefully a person tries to hide their feelings and experiences, things slip. We cannot conceal our inner mind fully because we communicate in many ways. Humans give off red flags or warning signs that something is wrong. Often we betray ourselves with our outward expressions and emotions that others can catch onto if they are trained and alert. A good friend will notice when things are different. A very good friend will find out what is wrong and help you help yourself. For Cliff, the very good friend was a person he worked with, and getting him help meant alerting military leadership that Cliff needed help. Cliff, however, being old-fashioned, did not appreciate that at all! He had the too-common mentality that seeking help in the military for any type of behavioral problems or getting treatment will ruin a career.

In some cases, at least in the past, the apprehension was warranted. There is no privacy in the military. The command knows everyone's business, especially on active duty where all medical care is completed in military hospitals and clinics, and all medical records go through the military health system. The reserve and national guard components have different laws and resources. For the most part, they receive medical treatment in civilian hospitals with civilian insurance. However, they report current medical and behavioral health issues in annual periodic health assessments, which alert leadership to medical and behavioral health issues that may limit their readiness to deploy. Many reserve component service members keep their ailments quiet so as not to affect their deployability and their chance at promotion. Cliff's anger at the true friend that brought the issue up with leadership was seemingly justified because it could potentially affect his medical readiness rating if he got help and received a profile that limited his ability to deploy. Readiness to deploy is the most significant status military leaders track for their commands and units. If a service member cannot deploy at any time, they are not an asset to their command.

Humans are limited in our decision-making because we believe our assumptions without investigating them before we make important decisions. There are paradoxes in life where the results of actions seem backwards. Spending less time with some people might result in better relationships with them. Taking a break from your work may make you a better employee. And seeking help for a behavioral or emotional problem may help your career instead of hurting it. Service members believe and assume that getting involved in treatment will hurt their deployability, reputation with leadership, and end up harming their career. The shared way of thinking is that reaching out for help is a sign of weakness and going public, be it to your leadership or just getting into in the system as someone seeking help, will hurt your reputation, perceived stability, or even security clearance and career outlook. However, without help, you cannot get better, and your career gets worse. By getting help, which is thought to harm your career, you are actually saving your career. The contradictory nature of things we hear and believe about seeking help versus what is actually true about it illustrate the need to dispel myths through education and training. Getting help saved Cliff's career—and his life.

Cliff initially saw psychologists as an enemy who could ruin his security clearance and end his career. He did not open up to them, and he did not get better. His doctors gave him sleeping and anti-anxiety medications but did not address the deeper set of issues that plagued him. He believed that seeking help would hurt his security clearance and interfere with his chances at promotion. In the end, it did not hurt his promotion, but actually helped him become a better soldier and a better man. He was promoted alongside his peers while receiving treatment and his security clearance was unaffected.

Psychotherapy and other treatment techniques have been validated by scientific studies. Treatment has nothing to do with weakness. Like any other type of health care, it supports a person's overall health and wellness. Physical and mental health need to be in balance, and our society needs to welcome that truth that so the millions of cases like Cliff's do not progress to suicidal attempts and loss of life. Therapy does not need to be reactionary, as it is part of the comprehensive feedback loop of preparing, reacting, and recovering from difficulty. Therapy helps us prepare for future difficulty, as the lessons we learn from our experiences can help us prepare for future events. We can learn to deal with things before they happen just as much as we can after they happen. Much like nurses learn to protect their backs through proper lifting techniques, we all need to learn to protect our mental health by learning productive ways to cope with stress as part of our overall well-being.

Cliff talks a lot about how therapy saved his life and how it continues to make him a better person. He was never officially diagnosed with any specific disorder. However, through counseling, he found ways to deal with his depressive ways, PTSD symptoms, and tendency to use alcohol to escape. He did it without medication. When Cliff feels himself start to go down a destructive path, he has skills now to avoid it. The road that led to a suicide attempt now has various off-ramps. He can make his own adjustments or find help from a therapist. When he meets people who have similar experiences with trauma and are at risk of suicide, he makes sure they receive the help they need to keep a "molehill just a molehill," and never let it grow into a mountain. His driving force is to help people avoid suicide. He has learned different techniques through his therapy and army resilience training. He now faces his nightmares, instead of avoiding sleep to avoid them. His mind is running a good program now, thanks to the help he sought.

CHAPTER 26

WHEREVER HE IS NOW, I WISH HIM ALL THE BEST

AFTER THE THIRD DAY OF SEARCHING for survivors, Bob Hewett returned home where his wife wanted to know what was going on and what he had been doing. She would not let him come inside the house with his dirty clothes and made him strip down with neighbors looking at him. It was awkward, but he did it for her. Three months after 9/11, the couple sold the house and moved back to their home state of Rhode Island.

The night he returned from responding to the Pentagon after the 9/11 attack, Jack went straight to his back yard and knocked on the sliding glass window. Asking his wife to bring out a trash bag, he removed every piece of noxious clothing—permeated with jet fuel, smoke from reigniting fires and hot spots, and all of the horror—and threw them all in the trash bag. He disposed of the trash bag after taking multiple showers.

The three did not maintain a physical relationship, and to this day, they have only been together as a group twice, first on 9/11 and the other time at a one-year anniversary of the attack, where a large group of Pentagon 9/11 first responders met at a steakhouse in the Northern Virginia area. Cliff, Jack, Bob, the AT&T accounts manager, Jared, and Walter also attended the event. They picked a nickname for their group: "The Cell Phone Warriors." Other than that, they exchanged emails and shared funny videos over the internet or other noncritical communication, but they did not get together outside of those two instances. Maybe they were avoiding memories of the event by not meeting up.

Cliff, Jack, and Bob all received the Army Commendation Medal for their response on 9/11, crawling through the rubble of the area of the Pentagon hit by Flight 77.

Cliff's citation, like the others, reads:

> For meritorious achievement through his selfless and tireless efforts to locate and rescue victims from the 11 September 2001 Pentagon tragedy. CW2 Bauman voluntarily crawled on his hands, knees, and belly through Pentagon rubble searching for survivors. CW2 Bauman's accomplishments reflect great credit upon himself and the United States Army.

Cliff was a keynote speaker at an event at the Association of the United States Army (AUSA) and, after a tour, ended up in the library talking to the librarian where he mentioned his story and the medals, as well as the uniform he had worn on 9/11. The librarian was interested in his story and believed she could help coordinate adding Cliff's items to the museum as a display. She got him in contact with the museum historian, and they made a deal for him to donate his items. His story has been seen by many visitors to the DC building, including a surprised Bob Hewett, who was not aware of any of the events in Cliff's life after 9/11.

In May 2019, Bob was at an AUSA event at the US Army Headquarters and was talking with another soldier, who asked him if he wanted to go see the museum on the bottom floor of the building. They walked downstairs to the museum, and the first thing Bob saw as he rounded the corner was a display with a uniform and boots and various pictures of Cliff, including his Soldier's Medal. He was flabbergasted and told the other soldier the story about that day. He was astonished to see it, and he emailed Jack. Jack replied that he had not seen it either. They were not aware of the other things that happened to Cliff, the suicide attempt, getting treatment, saving the sailors' lives, and becoming a leader in the fight against suicide in the military.

All three eventually deployed in support of the response to the attacks, either in Operation Iraqi Freedom or Operation Enduring Freedom in Afghanistan. Bob was an Air National Guardsman during the 9/11 attack on the Pentagon and deployed in support of Operation Iraqi Freedom. He was based out of Germany, but flew missions into Kosovo, former Yugoslavia, Italy,

Iraq, Turkey, Afghanistan, Kazakhstan, and into Liberia, where he helped evacuate the embassy staff during the Liberian civil war. A tradition in the military during wartime deployment is to fly a flag over the combat zone in the name of friends, family, or battle buddies. Later on, you give them the flag, along with a certificate of flight in their name. Bob flew a flag over Afghanistan for his 9/11 colleagues, Jack and Cliff. After his enlistment was up, Cliff and others convinced him to cross over into the Army National Guard, ending his enlisted service and gaining a commission as a Warrant Officer. He ran into Jack during warrant officer training school. Jack was an official in the school and was happy to see Bob—especially in an Army uniform! They drank into the night.

Jack worked in a different section at the NGB's headquarters than Cliff did, although they stayed in contact. Being a data processing warrant officer, Jack was really good with computers and databases. After the attack, Operation Iraqi Freedom commenced. Jack repeatedly requested to deploy. His leadership wanted him to stay at the bureau headquarters in Crystal City, Virginia, but he persisted and ended up getting the Iraq deployment he wanted. When his deployment was granted, a Colonel in his command stated, "Well, I hope you are happy, you got what you wanted." Jack faced resistance from his organization, but it did not stop him from seeking operational experience. Jack knew that his work at home was important, but he knew his service in Iraq would be even more valuable.

In Iraq, Jack often traveled with the Reserve Component Division Commander, Colonel Paul Kelly. They were regularly on the same flights in Iraq, and they became friends. In November 2006, Jack's request to extend his stay was denied. The NGB needed him back to fulfill his promise to take over as the executive officer—a deal he had made to go on deployment in the first place. On January 20, 2007, two months after Jack left Iraq, Colonel Kelly was killed at the age of 45 when he was flying back from Baghdad. He was among twelve soldiers to die in the crash, which claimed ten national guard soldiers and two active-duty soldiers. Jack states that Colonel Kelly was a great guy; he would give you the shirt off his back. He had a wife and two sons. Jack believes that he would have been with Colonel Kelly if he had been permitted to extend his stay. Colonel Kelly lives on in the memories of his battle buddies like Jack, as well as his family and friends, as do thousands of other service members who have made the ultimate sacrifice in the contingency operations following 9/11.

In another case of fate intermingling with chance, a major from the National Guard was supposed to be on the trip that day and had just returned from another trip. He asked Colonel Kelly if he could fly with them, but Colonel Kelly looked at him and said, "You look real tired Major, you will make the next flight." That man just missed being on the helicopter. He got a tattoo with the names of all the soldiers on the flight that day. He had the same sense of survivor's guilt that Cliff experienced, feeling like he should have been on the flight.

"Wherever he is now, I wish him all the best." Then Jack says again, "The mind is a complicated computer."

In 2006, Jack was assigned to the Multi-National Corps Iraq headquarters, personnel division. He worked diligently for the division, using his computer programming skills to re-write Corps-level databases. He created a much-needed personnel records keeping system. His group was also charged with determining which local Iraqis should receive US technology and Iraqi headquarters personnel kits. This task required collecting biometric data from all Iraqi soldiers. Jack was part of a team charged with balancing all of the information, including DNA, voice scans, fingerprints, palm prints, and all sorts of biometric data to help the Coalition Forces know which side the Iraqi soldiers were on—for lack of a better way to put it. They developed what they called the Unit Transition Point (UTP) team to collect this data.

The UTP team distributed jump kits with biometric data collection equipment, including cameras, scanners, etc., throughout the country. They collected data from criminals previously released by Sadaam Hussein's prisons. The idea was that these released prisoners or other individuals could try to undermine the new Iraqi Army by joining it and then bringing down morale or perpetrating acts of violence. Tracking them could preclude insider attacks. Their fear came true, and insider attacks became common. Jack and his team weeded these personnel out of the Iraqi Army with their system. They rehearsed the plan thousands of times with local Iraqi translators and built a strong information network and database. The program took Jack and his team all around Iraq. Another officer who was at the Pentagon on 9/11 was the other UTP team leader. He and Jack split up the work, and each led one team throughout the area of responsibility to collect data to mitigate insider threats in the new Iraqi Army.

The term "Anbar Awakening" refers to a time when local Sunni Sheikhs started to cooperate with US and Coalition Forces in western Iraq—the Anbar Province—in its fight against al-Qaeda. The large area was controlled by al-Qaeda, but with the help of local Iraqis, Iraqi security forces, and the United States, al-Qaeda was removed from the region. The Anbar Awakening became a prototype for future operations working with local security forces and local populations in safeguarding regions and advancing order, safety, control, and a way ahead for a new government. The UTP mission was an integral part of the Anbar Awakening. Jack was awarded the OIF Campaign Medal, a Joint Service Commendation Medal, and a Bronze Star for his service in Iraq.

Jack requested to deploy many more times after his time in Iraq but was denied every time. He retired from the military in 2012. Part of his decision was based on his desire to work in an operational environment. This was extremely important to him and being denied the opportunity to deploy was frustrating. Upon retiring, Jack took command of the United States Warrant Officer's Association as the National Executive Director of the association. He is also president of the military coalition, which includes the AUSA, Air Force Association, Veterans of Foreign Wars, Wounded Warrior Project, National Guard Association of the United States, Enlisted Association of the National Guard of the United States, and all of the big military associations in

Washington, DC. Jack has spoken in front of Capitol Hill to advocate for military benefits, representing 5.5 million service members, with all of the combined associations. The coalition has passed important bills for the military, and Jack is a member of many boards and operates in an executive status.

CHAPTER 27

PLEASE DON'T CALL ME EVERY TIME YOU SEE A MAN WEARING SKINNY SHORTS

CLIFF HAD KEPT AGENT SMITH'S PHONE number from the 9/11 anniversary event. You never know when having an FBI agent's phone number will come in handy. It happened to do so a few weeks after the get-together. The NGB building had the highest concentration of general officers of any building in the DC metropolitan area—generals from different agencies who were forced to move from the Pentagon during the renovation. It would be a rich target for an attack. Soldiers are observant and believe in the expression, "See Something, Say Something." It is a code to enhance our situational awareness and guides us in protecting our own. Now, Cliff noticed a strange situation where a man was sitting on the top of the Crowne

Plaza hotel across from the NGB, wearing skinny shorts and a t-shirt, observing the National Guard building, through binoculars. He called Jack.

"Hey Jack, there is a strange person watching the NGB building."

"What makes him strange?"

"Well, he is wearing skinny shorts."

"Well, that is odd, but does not make him strange."

"How about the fact that he is also watching the entrances through binoculars."

"Okay, now that raises the situation from odd to suspicious."

"What do you think we should do?"

"Well, we gotta let somebody know."

"How about that Agent Smith fella?"

"Well, that is a good start!"

Cliff called Agent Smith.

Cliff, Jack, and another soldier sat across from the NGB headquarters, Jack smoking a cigarette, Cliff watching the binoculars man. Agent Smith was a connected, effective agent. Within minutes, three black government Suburbans pulled up and escorted the man away, and that was that—or at least the end of their involvement in the situation.

Well, for Jack, "that was that" was not enough. It was a suspicious and disturbing situation, and he did not want to let it sit at that, without a follow-up. Through a little investigating on his own, he found out just enough to make him glad he reported the man, though he was unable to get the full story.

Jack found his lead in the form of a lawyer he knew. "Do you know anything about the case of the man who was spotted suspiciously observing the NGB building entrances?"

"Hmm, I remember hearing something about it, but can't really tell you anything."

"Well, I was the person who called it in and was interested in a little follow-up. Are we in any danger? What did they find out about the guy?"

"Wait, you were the one who reported him? Well, I guess I owe it to you to tell you what I know. We were questioning him and found out that he was the American-born son of nationalized Lebanese parents, who were in the country. Funny thing is, the man is actually a full-time member of the military!"

"Wait, really? Where is he now?"

"Well, Jack, he basically disappeared into the system. We don't know what he was doing, and he may be answering questions to another agency now, but he is out of our hands. I guess we will never know what was going on in his mind while he was watching your building."

"Well, I will keep my eyes out for a man wearing skinny shorts and give you a call so you can finish your investigation."

"Jack, please don't call me every time you see a man wearing skinny shorts." They both winced and then smiled.

CHAPTER 28

HUNTING THE GOOD STUFF

CLIFF OWES HIS LIFE TO AN incredible call to his brother's work, a call that went directly to a desk line in a different part of the hospital from where he normally worked, in a fortunate coincidence. He owes his later success in life to family and social support, therapy, and the resilience skills he learned in the army. The recovery after his suicide attempt made him change his mind about therapy and counseling, and he became an advocate for mental health services. In hundreds of interactions, he has changed the minds of countless others who were struggling with finding a reason to live. His message is that therapy does not make you a weaker person; it makes you a stronger person. Cliff and the army's efforts to erase the stigma of seeking professional help for mental and mood concerns are paying off, as office visits to counselors have increased at a high rate in the years following the end to the Iraq war. For example, the number of soldiers seeking help at one Northern Virginia army base went from less than four thousand office visits in 2008 to around twelve thousand visits in 2012.[81]

There is a contagion effect that surrounds mental health. It can be good, or it can be bad. Many people would be worse off without Cliff's influence. Certainly, many people of those who were impacted by him to seek help would not be around. The three boaters would not have been saved from drowning. Many others, both in the military and civilian communities, have benefitted through the chain of events in Cliff's life. His personal decision to seek help led to a contagion effect, inspiring others affected by trauma to search for help and reasons to live. Talking about his experiences is painful, but he knows that if he can help people avoid the path of suicide, his efforts will be well worth it.

For years Cliff Bauman recounted his dangerous and selfless rescue efforts in the Chesapeake Bay to colleagues, family, friends, reporters, and in front of a large group of people, but he never brought up his struggles with PTSD and depression. He certainly did not ever mention his suicide attempt. It would be a long time before he ever went public about those parts of his life. Telling that part of the story would take encouragement.

The University of Pennsylvania is well known for its research in resilience and positive psychology. It helped the army develop the Master Resilience Training (MRT) program to develop soldiers' coping skills to make them stronger and more resilient in the face of life-changing events. Soldiers attend a standardized ten-day course to become a certified MRT trainer. When they go back to their unit, they coach other soldiers to help build their resilience through lessons based on the MRT curriculum. Ten years after 9/11, Cliff attended the full course at the University of Pennsylvania to become a certified trainer. It was not voluntary for him, as he was "voluntold" to attend the course. He went somewhat begrudgingly, not knowing that it would change his life's trajectory.

Chief Bauman did well in the course. He participated when he felt like it. Then, everything aligned one day, and he finally spoke up about his personal experience with PTSD, survivor's guilt, and suicide, something he had never done. His testimony brought the empathetic group of students to tears, as many of them had endured similar trauma but kept it private. Some students talked with him after the class. They encouraged him to share his story with others because it could help people overcome obstacles in their life that were holding them back from seeking help. That was what he needed to hear. Cliff decided to share his story in hopes that he could make a difference. Word of his story spread, opening opportunities for him to share his message. He started speaking to small groups.

Cliff's message was making an impact. His leadership knew about his speaking and his reputation as a suicide prevention speaker started to grow on base. During a meeting at his command headquarters, the Chief of Staff for Personnel told a group of leaders that the Department of Veterans Affairs (VA) was looking to record videos about mental health in the military and to find out from their soldiers if any of them wanted to be a part of it. Cliff's supervisor told him about it, and Cliff got involved with the VA, making his first of many successful military mental health and suicide prevention videos. The video received thousands of views and positive comments, and it effectively opened the door for his public speaking appearances. At the time, he was the only active-duty officer to speak publicly about a suicide attempt. When the video was released, it was the highest-grossing video to date for the program.

Through countless speaking events, as well as newspaper, magazine, and video platforms, Cliff grew as an influential public speaker and suicide prevention professional. At first his leadership did not totally support him making videos and getting involved in events or campaigns for various reasons. He had to use his paid leave to travel and do speaking engagements for the military and pay his own room and travel expenses. Traditionally, military training is funded by military lines of accounting that are earmarked for travel to and from training, as well as lodging and a per diem for food and essential items. For the VA video, he had to self-fund it.

Cliff retired from the army in 2022. Prior to his retirement, as an active-duty soldier, he could not charge an honorarium or speaking fee when he did military events. However, after a legal review, his command eventually started to allow the requesting organizations to fund his trips with unit money, though they could not pay him for his time. He jokes that he was the world's cheapest public speaker, and it is more than a joke as speakers of his caliber charge hefty fees to do the same type of presentation for a military audience. During his active-duty time, his audience ranged from the brand-new enlisted private to the most seasoned three- or four-star general.

In his talks, Cliff covers many subjects, personalized depending on his audience, the reactions he receives, and what he knows to be common issues with the members or at the location. He meets with commanders before an engagement to determine the context of the event. He often speaks about good leaders versus bad leaders. He reports that he was treated very badly by some of his leaders after making the video. Stigma was still high at the time, and he was going against the rules, becoming the first high-profile soldier to speak out against stigma in the military over help-seeking and suicide prevention. However, that pushback did not stop him from continuing his mission. For him, it was important enough to continue. And things got better.

Military leadership support for Cliff gained steam, and eventually he had his leaders' support for what he was doing. They did not actively advertise his events, but they no longer stood in the way or denied him receiving travel funding for trips to speak to large groups of soldiers about mental health and suicide prevention topics. In fact, many of his leaders and commanders have become big advocates of his training events.

Cliff talks with military service members about his story. He also talks with their family members and even their children. With children, he talks about different topics such as life in the military, serving in Iraq, and the importance of a supporting family. Depending on their age, he can talk about suicide prevention. He speaks to civilians as well, in many different venues, ranging from small college classrooms to large-scale organizational events. Sometimes his audience includes only students and sometimes the audience is the population at-large. He adapts to each audience, going into detail about different aspects of his story depending on his listeners and the event. No matter the group, he finds a way to connect, as that is the main purpose of his speaking. After making a connection, he can answer questions and address what the audience needs. And he can talk offline to individuals from the group about different topics.

Cliff does not need time to put his presentations together, as he can speak extemporaneously. He never misses an opportunity to spread the message of mental health treatment as suicide prevention. There are many examples of him taking advantage of a situation to get in front of a group and lead a discussion. In one case, while in Hawaii supporting an army mission, Cliff and his group were talking with a chaplain on the local army base. The chaplain was having a prayer breakfast for about seventy people. Hearing Cliff's story of hope, the chaplain asked if he would come to speak for the group, and Cliff was happy to oblige him and the group, even though it was during a working trip. He gave the only few hours he would have had to himself during that part of the trip, missing out on sightseeing with other members of the group. Another act of the selfless service that he has shown throughout his career. The event was a success, and he rejoined the group later that day without making a big deal about what he had done that morning. Cliff is all in for the cause, no matter what free time he must sacrifice.

Being a soldier today means attending a lot of time-consuming mandatory training, most often online in the form of a PowerPoint slideshow lecture. In the past, the same training was accomplished in small sections, led by squad-level leaders. It was interactive and quick. After the training, the unit resumed "army work." Trainings became more formalized, to the dismay of leaders that would prefer a more personal and informal training approach. Changes have been made to allow more latitude for the commander to decide what training is necessary for the unit and what training is not as necessary, but the training mode remains computer based. It is easy now to read from a slide to a group of service members. However, good presenters know how to use slides and pictures for emphasis, and to let the content come from the speaker. With a picture of his family on the screen, Cliff gets teary-eyed while telling his story, as his sons would never have been born if he had died during his suicide attempt. Very often, the crowd gets teary-eyed too. The evaluations are always good, as military members appreciate the authenticity of a compelling personal story.

Public speaking is an outlet for Cliff Bauman, and he gives a lot of himself through speaking to help others. It is reciprocal, though, as he gets a lot out of it as well. He tells his story of hope to warn people not to go down the same path as he did. Learned experience suicide prevention promotion is the best type of suicide prevention. Giving his personal example of a good, positive story lets him work through his pain and suffering, knowing that maybe someone out in the audience is going through the very same things and that they will be motivated to seek help. If he can change one person's mind, help just one listener realize it is okay to ask for help, his mission is accomplished, and the long arduous process of planning, traveling, and speaking has served its purpose.

Cliff speaking at one of his many events. Photo credit: Clifford Bauman.

It is a humbling experience to see your name and story in the press. Cliff is humbled every time he does a video or an article. He wants to help other soldiers by speaking and writing and doing the things he does.

However, it takes a toll on him emotionally and physically. Still, he feels it is important to get his story out and show people that there is hope. He wants people to know that bad things can happen to people in their lives, or things may not necessarily go the way they should go, and it is okay—we just need to learn how to deal with it in a positive manner as much as we can. Listening to his speeches, you will hear many motivating statements.

"At some given time in each of our lives, we will all need help. Life is full of trials and is not perfect, and it is okay to seek help. You do not have to go through it alone and seeking help does not make you less of a person or less of a man, a father, mother, or anything else. On the contrary, it will make you a better person altogether if you can address your problems effectively."

As difficult and time-consuming it is to prepare, travel, and do a speaking event, Cliff enjoys it. After every speaking engagement, members of the audience come up to him and either thank him for his wisdom or give him a hug and tell him they appreciate him telling his story. And every time, one or more of them tell him their own story of a traumatic event they have experienced or their personal story relating to suicide. In any large gathering of people, you can be sure that at least one person in the crowd has had experiences with suicide. A sensitive public figure is a magnet for people to approach with their own stories. At this point, he has heard thousands of personal stories, untold to anyone else.

Whether he is speaking to soldiers or civilians, or to newspapers or other news outlets, he feels that the answers all regard the same issues—stigma associated with mental health. It is something we must fight through. The path that he and others have gone through is not a good one; there are better ways, and he would prefer you take the better route. Instead of self-destruction, he would like you to find life, healing, and strength to deal with your situation. He would like you to find resilience. That is why he continues to do what he does. And he will do it for as long as he can.

As of 2022, Cliff has spoken in Germany, Korea, Hawaii, California, Minnesota, Michigan, Mississippi, Alabama, Tennessee, North and South Carolina, Washington, and other states and countries. In one trip to South Korea, he spoke at sixteen different suicide stand-down events on some of the numerous US military bases. It was an exhausting schedule, culminating in a suicide awareness 5K run, which he couldn't pass up, being an avid runner. He would find time to rest later!

There are numerous suicide prevention related organizations, and it is a small community. Cliff has made connections throughout the years and has been involved in many engagements and events. He routinely calls into teleconferences with various organizations and assists them in planning events with different organizations.

By 2017, Cliff was a well-known suicide prevention public speaker in the DoD community. DoD sources contacted Cliff to be a part of a DoD-VA coordinated suicide prevention conference to tell his story. Cliff accepted and spoke at the event in Denver, Colorado, in 2017. During that event, the promoters of the event thought up the idea to have a lived experience panel and invited Cliff to be a part of it. The promoters titled the discussion, the Life Worth Living Panel. From that panel, Cliff met the founder and several executive officers of Tragedy Assistance Program for Survivors (TAPS),[82] and the executive director of Suicide Awareness Voices of Education (SAVE).[83] After the event, the SAVE executive director invited Cliff to speak at a suicide prevention event at the US Capitol Building. The group wanted one military person to speak, and Cliff was the best fit for the event. Details would follow. Cliff did not know how large the event would be, but he would show up when and where they asked him.

In June 2019, on the SAVE executive director's recommendation, the National Council for Suicide Prevention invited Cliff to speak at the "Rally to Prevent Suicide" at the US Capitol building in DC. Cliff took an Uber from his work, getting as close as he could until the pedestrian traffic got too heavy. He climbed out of the Uber and joined a crowd of 750 people walking to the Capitol Building. Included in the group were many suicide survivors and family members and others supporting the cause.

As Cliff arrived and saw the large group, he did not know where he was supposed to be, just that it was with the marching group. He had attended the previous year as a member of the audience, but the location had moved. He ended up walking alongside a woman, just as "walking buddies," more or less. She told him about her son who died by suicide. She told Cliff about their relationship, his military career, the location, and its meaning to what had happened. She did not know his story or why he was there, just that he was safe to talk to. After they arrived at the location, Cliff told her goodbye and went on his way to find out where he was supposed to be. He pressed toward the front of the crowd and located his contact. Political figures and heads of various defense organizations and agencies gave speeches about their stories or about new policies in the works to fight suicide. However, Cliff gave the most memorable speech out of all of them.

Cliff speaking on Capitol Hill in 2019. Photo credit: Clifford Bauman.

One part of his speech that day had him "laying on the couch, dying by his own hand." The audience burst out in tears, and it was an amazing moment to have that connection with the audience. It was a five-minute speech, but the audience and reporters were touched. One article on the event reported this about Cliff's speech:

> "By far, the most moving speech of the event was delivered by Cliff Bauman, an Army chief warrant officer and suicide attempt survivor, who would have died by his own hand in 2002 had he not been rescued by his brother. Bauman told an emotionally powerful story of surviving the 9/11 attacks at the Pentagon, his subsequent PTSD and suicide attempt, and ultimately getting his career and life back on track. Today, Bauman is an accomplished career officer who speaks widely to audiences in the hopes of shedding light on the importance of getting help. As Bauman put it: 'We stand together today, at this moment, to tell the world it is OKAY NOT TO BE OKAY.'"[84]

Later, the woman he had walked with to the Capitol Building came up to him and gave him a hug. She asked why he did not tell her about his story or anything about being one of the speakers while they were walking and talking. He said he wanted to listen to her story without interrupting or putting himself into the situation. Sometimes when you are listening to someone, it is easy to put yourself into their story, but hard to take yourself out of it, so it is better to just listen.

The Capitol Building event was widely publicized. A news reporter from a media establishment in the Kurdistan region of Iraq, called RUDAW Media Network,[85] read about the event and contacted Cliff. They have done several media projects together, including two videos, a live TV panel, and two live interviews. Kurdistan has faced a suicide problem, and Cliff feels honored to help them with their program.

Another international event Cliff did was an interview with a group of college students from the Netherlands. The group reached out to him because they were working on a school project and came across his website. He did a telephone interview with them on September 10. Then, on September 11, Cliff spoke to a group of sixth graders from his hometown. He did not talk about his suicide attempt, but about his actions on 9/11. It was a great honor, and the students were excited because he had a similar background to them. Cliff grew up in a small town in Missouri, and he probably went to school with some of their parents! And here he was at the Pentagon during 9/11. The world outside seemed more accessible to them after talking with Cliff. They saw that success in the world outside their community is attainable if you are interested in pursuing it.

In 2020, a new health care and health news and information streaming website found Cliff and asked him if he would be part of a "Surviving Suicide" series. After negotiating and getting approvals, the documentary company drove out from California to start filming the project. The crew filmed Cliff speaking at an event in Wisconsin for the Wisconsin National Guard. The armory was also an aviation museum, similar to the Smithsonian aviation museum, but full of service members that day. It was a cold January day in 2020, and Cliff spoke to the large audience while the Able Channel film crew made their documentary.[86] After filming in Wisconsin, the unit returned and then two weeks later visited him at his home in Virginia for more filming. They lived with him and his family for ten days. They videotaped him and his family doing various daily routines, from life at work, to Krystal taking Junior to his wrestling practices and tournaments.

Then the film crew flew with Cliff to his brother's house in Kansas City, where he had attempted suicide many years ago. They visited Truman Medical Center, where his brother Dell had rushed him to after he took twenty-two sleeping pills in an attempt to end his own life. They interviewed his family, friends, and colleagues in various locations. The video was released on Veterans Day, November 11, 2020, and was a big success.

Cliff now hosts "The Mental Health Warrior" on Veteran Trash Talk network (VTT).[87] He was a guest on a VTT "Throatpunch Monday" podcast on YouTube, and it went very well. The VTT staff contacted him, asking if he wanted to have his own podcast on the VTT line-up. His podcast covers military and mental health aspects, including mind, body, and spiritual health. His guests include health professionals, doctors, trauma survivors, publishers, athletes, and everyday people with stories about confronting stigma and asking for help. He also appears on other podcasts.

Not all of Cliff's stories are about the Pentagon on 9/11, his suicide attempt, or saving lives from the capsized boat. He can recall many other times saving lives and many near-death experiences before and during his military service. When he was in his early twenties, Cliff came across an accident on a dark road in the middle of the countryside, where a major country road intersected a highway. A person hauling a horse trailer did not see the stop sign where it meets a T-junction into the highway, and T-boned another car, sending them both off a bridge. Both vehicles had gone into a massive ditch, about 10-12 feet deep.

When Cliff came upon the scene, two of the vehicle occupants had managed to escape their vehicle. However, one lady was still trapped inside. Cliff crawled down into the truck. She had a massive gash on her head. Head wounds bleed terribly, and he was administering first aid to her and was talking with her and keeping her calm. There was a two-year-old girl in the car who, luckily, had not been injured. The two horses had been ejected from the trailer, and both had to be put down. The lady was upset and concerned about the cut on her head, but Cliff was keeping her calm. He knew the cut was not too bad, and it was the amount of blood that normally comes from a head laceration.

Cliff had been trained to deal with traumatic injuries, and he was providing first aid. When people are injured and lose a significant amount of blood, their heart loses the ability to push blood throughout the body, resulting in hypovolemic shock. And when someone is injured in an accident that violently impacts their head or spine, special care is needed not to move their head or neck in order to avoid paralysis, or worse, death. Cliff held her head stationary as they sat on the side of the truck, waiting for the ambulance to arrive.

The ambulance finally arrived, and an EMT went down the hillside and the first words out of his mouth—after Cliff had been keeping her calm and stopping the bleeding for 45 minutes—were, "Oh Ma'am, you will need plastic surgery!" She immediately went into shock.

Cliff nearly went ballistic on him because of how thoughtless and insensitive this comment had been. He was yelling at the EMT, and a police officer had to restrain him.

Cliff was living with his younger sister and her husband at this time and had to shower the blood and mud off of himself. He was happy to find out that the lady ended up being fine. It was just a bad accident from a driver who was not from the area and not aware of the T-bone junction. Nobody was killed, and it could have been a lot worse.

Cliff had a near-death experience during his 33-week advanced individual training to become an aircraft armament repairman for the Cobra helicopter. His courses were in the night, and he had his days open. He started skydiving with a group of soldiers in a program run by a group of ex-Navy SEALs out of a local airport. On his second jump, the jumpmaster gave him the wrong parachute, and Cliff was not able to control it because it was too large.

During the fall, he had no control of where he was going, being at mercy of the wind. The jumpmaster came over the airwaves to Cliff's radio headset, stating, "remember what we said about tree landings?" Cliff had no reply but to yell a few choice words as he flared his parachute, bounced off in between two trees, and hit the ground. He was thrown into a sticker bush about a mile and a half from the airport, and his skydiving friends came running across, thinking Cliff was dead from the impact. He was not. He came crawling out of the bush—scratched up, but alive.

In another near-death experience, Cliff and his unit attended annual training in Germany in 1994. Cliff and his battle buddy Steve had the habit of telling each other their dreams, just for conversation. One night Cliff had a very strange, vivid dream, where the unit was late returning from their annual training trip in Germany, and they landed on a very cold island in the Atlantic Ocean. They crash landed, but everyone survived. He expanded on the details, including the faces of the aircrew. And it was amusing to them. The dream became a real-life nightmare about a week before the group left to return to Missouri. The unit was all in their seats about halfway through the flight when one of the aircrew members walked down the hallway. Now, Steve remembers that Cliff's face froze. Cliff flashed back to his dream, which started with that aircrew member's face. The aircrew prepared the aircraft, and the passengers prepared for a crash landing. The airplane was flying through a big Nor'easter, and the pilot had to radio into New York, and they were diverted to Gander, Newfoundland. The passengers moved around all items to the back of the aircraft to make it heavier and prepared for an ocean landing.

"Oh crap, my life raft is past its expiration date!"

"Well then when you pop it open, nothing but moths will come out!"

"Dammit, well I don't think it would do much anyway—look out the window."

Cliff and Steve looked out the window at the water below, creeping closer. An eerie silence settled over the airplane.

The KC-135 fuel tanker they were in landed in a snowstorm in Gander, Newfoundland. The pilot could not see the runway, so he had the runway lights way up high, and the pilot dropped the plane down as soon as he saw they were above the runway. The KC-135 plane landed hard and slid sideways down the runway, coming to rest about fifteen feet from the end.

The group exited the plane after their scary landing. Emergency vehicles lined the runway. The pilot was as white as a ghost, and his flight suit was soaking wet. But he got them all safely to the ground. Inside the terminal, in Gander, some of the soldiers went to the bar for a drink.

Cliff asked a woman working there, "Were you a little nervous about us coming to land here?"

She replied to him with a little grin on her face, "Nah, you guys need to crash here and refuel. No pun intended!"

"Oh well, I guess we are spending the night in Gander!"

The next morning the group ate breakfast in a cafeteria with the Royal Canadian Mounted Police. The food was excellent, but the ladies behind the counter were getting angry with them because they were not eating enough of it! That seemed funny to the group. After all, Cliff's group of soldiers was not running around the mountains all day like the mounted police! And they had Army height and weight standards and the Army Physical Fitness Test (APFT) to prepare for.

The unit commander got word of Cliff's dream. "So, Sergeant Bauman, did you have any more dreams last night?"

"No Sir," Cliff replied to the commander, "I think we had our near-death experience for this trip!"

These events are all part of Cliff's experience. Surviving his own near-death experiences was fate. Later in life, he changed other peoples' fates—that of the sailors who survived their accident because he put himself into their deadly water situation.

Fate is malleable. It is a construct humans developed to make sense of things that happen by chance, to give some sort of control over outcomes that were really just a matter of luck. We would be powerless without the belief in fate if we really confronted that nothing was ever set, and out of the millions of ways our lives could have turned out, it was "fate." Fate explains why it turned out this way. Really, it might also be chance. We believe in self-determination when our situations are driven by choices that we have control over. We believe in fate when outcomes are driven by chance. Responsibility lies in self-determination, and chance and luck lie in fate. What do we control and what does fate control?

You may believe fate is nothing more than chance, but does your mind follow along with that belief? When the question concerns traumatic experiences, the answer is a resounding "no" because of the disorderly nature of untreated PTSD. Perceptions are mixed-up and magical thinking leads people to believe they had more control of the outcome of a past event than they actually did. Survivor's guilt makes survivors and first responders question what they should have done differently, when they should instead be focusing on what they knew at the time. The senseless, purposeless martyrdom that takes good men and women's lives is rooted in symptoms of untreated, operative past trauma. There is a way to de-condition ourselves out of this destructive pattern. The first step is seeing the pattern objectively, from the outside. Through therapy and counseling, good men's and women's lives are saved as they understand past traumatic events and learn from them, becoming stronger and more resilient, rather than more self-destructive.

The journey of learning from past trauma takes the form of finding insight through questions and reflection. Firstly, are the negative or denial coping mechanisms that we adopt related to trauma we have experienced in our past? If so, would it be wise to learn how past trauma has affected our thinking and find a better way to cope with our memories? How is the event affecting us? Is it important to learn from our past? Why have we not

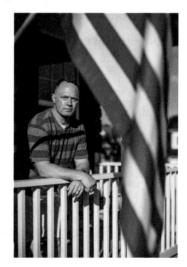

Photo credit: Shawn Hubbard Photography.

learned from our past? What is available to help us become more resilient? How can we internalize the changes in our thinking of our past trauma?

The events of September 11, 2001, created flashbulb memories for hundreds of millions of people—Americans and non-Americans alike. Mentioning 9/11 brings up difficult memories for people old enough to remember that tragic day. "Where were you on 9/11?" produces an evocative reply from many. For Cliff, his answer is fully positive and rational. He was doing what he always did. He was working to save lives and change others' fates. Since that date, he has been through a lot. He has transcended from guilt and hopelessness to ultimate redemption, and his public endorsement of the benefits of seeking help has saved untold thousands of lives.

Cliff knows firsthand how helpful it is to have someone trained to help us work things out. Through therapy we find positive solutions and perspective that we cannot see on our own. Years after his suicide attempt, Cliff no longer sees mental health treatment as a weakness. He understands that through therapy, survivors learn lessons from their experience instead of facing PTSD symptoms alone. Often there is no way of learning how to deal with these issues unless you seek help from a professional. Choosing to ask for help may be difficult, but it can mean the difference between life and death. Flashbacks and vivid dreams of traumatic events can come back at any time, but through counseling, survivors can contend with the invader. There is a bridge . . . from suicide . . . to hope.[88]

ACKNOWLEDGMENTS

MANY PEOPLE PROVIDED VALUABLE INFORMATION CENTRAL to telling this story with fidelity to the fine details. Firstly, thank you, Clifford Bauman. I appreciate your story of hope and what you do every day for the suicide prevention community. Robert Hewett, thank you for recounting your experience on 9/11 with such a keen eye for the technical details. Jack Du Teil, thank you for meeting with me, detailing your memories of 9/11, and sharing events that happened later because of the event. Dell Bauman, thank you for your interview and providing information about Cliff and his suicide attempt. I am thankful you were there that day and had a feeling something was not right. Sergeant Christopher King, thank you for sharing the training you go through as a police officer, and for your service as a first responder. FEMA Center for Domestic Preparedness cadre, thank you for sharing your resources for incident command in general, and for 9/11, specifically. Thank you, Jon Nichols from Norfolk Marine, for talking me through the details of your company. Lieutenant Colonel (retired) Robert Rossow III, I appreciate your communication and sending me a limited-run copy of your book *Uncommon Strength*—and sending a second copy when the first package arrived torn open and empty! Thank you, Colonel (retired) Ric Talley, for sharing your account of the events at the Pentagon on 9/11, and for taking us inside the War Room! Jose Mojica, thank you for your leadership in the Army Suicide Prevention Program and for putting me on many key developmental assignments for the five years I worked for you. Thank you to all suicide prevention professionals who I had the pleasure to work with in the past. Thank you to my mother, Judy, for walking me through the editing process and helping me with the bibliography and endnotes. Thank you to the many Pentagon 9/11 survivors who spoke with me and provided insight, though they chose to remain anonymous. Thanks to Lauren for your work in bringing this book through the publishing process, Cheryl for your careful editing, and Hobbs, Austin, Nina, and the rest of the Amplify team for your support navigating the publishing waters. And last, but most importantly, thank you to my family, who supported me when I spent extra time in my office during nights and weekends working on this book. Thank you to everyone mentioned here and for any that I may have overlooked for helping get this story out to the readers. You are all servant-leaders, and your contributions were indispensable not just to composing this book, but to the nation's defense, through your careers, in general.

—William D. Kammerer, Ph.D.

BIBLIOGRAPHY

"ABLE Channel." Accessed August 29, 2022. https://theablechannel.com/.

Acosta, Joie D., Amariah Becker, Jennifer L. Cerully, Michael P. Fisher, Laurie T. Martin, Raffaele Vardavas, Mary Ellen Slaughter, and Terry L. Schell. "Assessing the Department of Defense's Approach to Reducing Mental Health Stigma." *RAND Corporation*, January 18, 2016. https://www.rand.org/pubs/research_briefs/RB9881.html.

Allen, Joseph A., Roni Reiter-Palmon, John Crowe, and Cliff Scott. "Debriefs: Teams Learning from Doing in Context." *The American Psychologist* 73, no. 4 (June 2018): 504–16. https://doi.org/10.1037/amp0000246.

American Psychiatric Association. *Diagnostic and Statistical Manual of Mental Disorders*. 4th ed., 1994.

American Psychiatric Association. *Diagnostic and Statistical Manual of Mental Disorders*. 5th ed. American Psychiatric Association, 2013. https://doi.org/10.1176/appi.books.9780890425596.

"ARD: Master Resilience Training." Accessed September 28, 2021. https://www.armyresilience.army.mil/ard/R2/Master-Resilience-Training.html.

"Arlington County Conference Report." Arlington, VA. 2003. https://arlingtonva.s3.amazonaws.com/wp-content/uploads/sites/21/2014/04/2012-ARCO_Conf_Report.pdf.

Bauer, Patricia. "American Airlines Flight 77 | Facts & History | Britannica," September 4, 2022. https://www.britannica.com/event/American-Airlines-flight-77.

Bauman, Clifford. "The Mental Health Warrior." 2022. https://cliffordbauman.com.

Baumel, W. Thomas, and John N. Constantino. "Implementing Logotherapy in Its Second Half-Century: Incorporating Existential Considerations Into Personalized Treatment of Adolescent Depression." *Journal of the American Academy of Child & Adolescent Psychiatry* 59, no. 9 (September 2020): 1012–15. https://doi.org/10.1016/j.jaac.2020.06.006.

Bolton, Sorcha, and Oliver J. Robinson. "The Impact of Threat of Shock-Induced Anxiety on Memory Encoding and Retrieval." *Learning & Memory* 24, no. 10 (October 2017): 532–42. https://doi.org/10.1101/lm.045187.117.

Brancu, Mira, Monica Mann-Wrobel, Jean C. Beckham, H. Ryan Wagner, Alyssa Elliott, Allison T. Robbins, Madrianne Wong, Ania E. Berchuck, and Jennifer J. Runnals. "Subthreshold Posttraumatic Stress Disorder: A Meta-Analytic Review of DSM-IV Prevalence and a Proposed DSM-5 Approach to Measurement." *Psychological Trauma: Theory, Research, Practice and Policy* 8, no. 2 (March 2016): 222–32. https://doi.org/10.1037/tra0000078.

Bratina, Michele P., Jacqueline A. Carsello, Kelly M. Carrero, and Michael E. Antonio. "An Examination of Crisis Intervention Teams in Rural Jurisdictions." *Community Mental Health Journal* 57, no. 7 (October 2021): 1388–98. https://doi.org/10.1007/s10597-021-00797-7.

Bratina, Michele P., Kelly M. Carrero, Bitna Kim, and Alida V. Merlo. "Crisis Intervention Team Training: When Police Encounter Persons with Mental Illness." *Police Practice and Research* 21, no. 3 (May 3, 2020): 279–96. https://doi.org/10.1080/15614263.2018.1484290.

Bryan, Mark L., Andrew M. Bryce, and Jennifer Roberts. "The Effect of Mental and Physical Health Problems on Sickness Absence." *The European Journal of Health Economics* 22, no. 9 (December 2021): 1519–33. https://doi.org/10.1007/s10198-021-01379-w.

Cameron, Heather A., and Timothy J. Schoenfeld. "Behavioral and Structural Adaptations to Stress." *Frontiers in Neuroendocrinology* 49 (April 2018): 106–13. https://doi.org/10.1016/j.yfrne.2018.02.002.

"Clifford Bauman – Recipient." Accessed November 21, 2020. http://valor.militarytimes.com/hero/33606.

Creed, Patrick, and Rick Newman. *Firefight: Inside the Battle to Save the Pentagon on 9/11.* New York: Presidio Press/Ballantine Books, 2008.

Cukor, Judith, Katarzyna Wyka, Brittany Mello, Megan Olden, Nimali Jayasinghe, Jennifer Roberts, Cezar Giosan, Michael Crane, and JoAnn Difede. "The Longitudinal Course of PTSD among Disaster Workers Deployed to the World Trade Center Following the Attacks of September 11th." *Journal of Traumatic Stress* 24, no. 5 (October 2011): 506–14. https://doi.org/10.1002/jts.20672.

Davies, Graham. "Book Review: Handbook of Eyewitness Psychology. Volume 1. Memory for Events," *Applied Cognitive Psychology* 21, no. 8 (December 2007): 1113–14. https://doi.org/10.1002/acp.1397.

Deak, Maryann C. and Robert Stickgold. "Sleep and Cognition." *WIREs Cognitive Science* 1, no. 4 (July 2010): 491–500. https://doi.org/10.1002/wcs.52.

Dietch, Jessica R., Camilo J. Ruggero, Keke Schuler, Daniel J. Taylor, Benjamin J. Luft, and Roman Kotov. "Posttraumatic Stress Disorder Symptoms and Sleep in the Daily Lives of World Trade Center Responders." *Journal of Occupational Health Psychology* 24, no. 6 (December 2019): 689–702. https://doi.org/10.1037/ocp0000158.

DVIDS. "Retired Army General, Wife Share Story of Loss." Accessed June 4, 2020. https://www.dvidshub.net/news/113713/retired-army-general-wife-share-story-loss.

DVIDS. "Suicide Prevention PSA: CSA Raymond T. Odierno." Accessed June 4, 2020. https://www.dvidshub.net/video/154428/suicide-prevention-psa-csa-raymond-t-odierno.

DVIDS. "Suicide Prevention PSA: SMA Raymond Chandler." Accessed June 4, 2020. https://www.dvidshub.net/video/154430/suicide-prevention-psa-sma-raymond-chandler.

Ellis, Horace A. "Effects of a Crisis Intervention Team (CIT) Training Program Upon Police Officers Before and After Crisis Intervention Team Training." *Archives of Psychiatric Nursing* 28, no. 1 (February 2014): 10–16. https://doi.org/10.1016/j.apnu.2013.10.003.

Federal Bureau of Investigation. "World Trade Center Bombing 1993." Accessed November 29, 2021. https://www.fbi.gov/history/famous-cases/world-trade-center-bombing-1993.

Feldman, Talya R., Caryn L. Carlson, Leslie K. Rice, Marc I. Kruse, Christopher G. Beevers, Michael J. Telch, and Robert A. Josephs. "Factors Predicting the Development of Psychopathology among First Responders: A Prospective, Longitudinal Study." *Psychological Trauma: Theory, Research, Practice, and Policy* 13, no. 1 (January 2021): 75–83. https://doi.org/10.1037/tra0000957.

Figley, Charles R., ed. *Brief Treatments for the Traumatized: A Project of the Green Cross Foundation.* Contributions in Psychology, no. 39. Westport, Conn: Greenwood Press, 2002.

Fimiani, Ramona, Francesco Gazzillo, Nino Dazzi, and Marshall Bush. "Survivor Guilt: Theoretical, Empirical, and Clinical Features." *International Forum of Psychoanalysis* 31, no. 3 (July 3, 2022): 176–90. https://doi.org/10.1080/0803706X.2021.1941246.

"Foreign Terrorists in America." Accessed June 29, 2020. https://irp.fas.org/congress/1998_hr/s980224c.htm.

"Fort Monroe After Base Realignment and Closure (BRAC)." Accessed November 21, 2020. http://www.virginiaplaces.org/military/fortmonroebrac.html.

Frankl, Viktor E., William J. Winslade, and Harold S. Kushner. *Man's Search for Meaning.* Translated by Helen Pisano and Ilse Lasch. Boston, Mass.: Beacon Press, 2015.

Garibbo, Michele, Jessica Aylward, and Oliver J Robinson. "The Impact of Threat of Shock-Induced Anxiety on the Neural Substrates of Memory Encoding and Retrieval." *Social Cognitive and Affective Neuroscience* 14, no. 10 (October 1, 2019): 1087–96. https://doi.org/10.1093/scan/nsz080.

Giacomantonio, Chris, Stephanie Goodwin, and Garland Carmichael. "Learning to De-Escalate: Evaluating the Behavioural Impact of Verbal Judo Training on Police Constables." *Police Practice and Research* 21, no. 4 (July 3, 2020): 401–17. https://doi.org/10.1080/15614263.2019.1589472.

Gilmartin, R. and S. Southwick. "Combat-Related PTSD and Logotherapy." *International Forum for Logotherapy*, 2004.

Goldberg, Alfred, Sarandis Papadopoulos, Diane Putney, Nancy Berlage, and Rebecca Welch. *Pentagon 9/11.* Defense Studies Series. Washington, DC: Historical Office, Office of the Secretary of Defense, 2007.

Hacker, Robyn L. and John J. Horan. "Policing People with Mental Illness: Experimental Evaluation of Online Training to de-Escalate Mental Health Crises." *Journal of Experimental Criminology* 15, no. 4 (December 2019): 551–67. https://doi.org/10.1007/s11292-019-09380-3.

Henderson, William. "Changes to the Security Clearance Mental Health Question." *ClearanceJobs*, July 6, 2013. https://news.clearancejobs.com/2013/07/06/changes-to-the-security-clearance-mental-health-question/.

History.com Editors. "World Trade Center Is Bombed." *HISTORY.* Accessed August 28, 2019. https://www.history.com/this-day-in-history/world-trade-center-bombed.

Huang, Garry, Tso-Ying Lee, Kondwani Joseph Banda, Li-Chung Pien, Hsiu-Ju Jen, Ruey Chen, Doresses Liu, Shu-Tai Shen Hsiao, and Kuei-Ru Chou. "Prevalence of Sleep Disorders among First Responders for Medical Emergencies: A Meta-Analysis." *Journal of Global Health* 12 (October 20, 2022): 04092. https://doi.org/10.7189/jogh.12.04092.

Hunnicutt-Ferguson, Kallio, Katarzyna E. Wyka, Melissa Peskin, Judith Cukor, Megan Olden, and JoAnn Difede. "Posttraumatic Stress Disorder, Functional Impairment, and Subjective Distress in World Trade Center Disaster Workers: PTSD and Impairment in Disaster Workers." *Journal of Traumatic Stress* 31, no. 2 (April 2018): 234–43. https://doi.org/10.1002/jts.22268.

ICC. "Today in History: World Trade Center Is Bombed." Accessed November 29, 2020. https://www.iccsafe.org/building-safety-journal/bsj-dives/today-in-history-world-trade-center-is-bombed/.

Intelligence Resource Program. "1999 Congressional Hearings." *Federation of American Scientists*, 2000. https://irp.fas.org/congress/1999_hr/index.html.

Joiner, Thomas E. *Why People Die by Suicide*. Cambridge, Mass: Harvard University Press, 2005.

Joint Base Langley-Eustis. "'Freedom's Fortress' Deactivated after 188 Years of Service." Accessed November 21, 2020. https://www.jble.af.mil/News/Article-Display/Article/258576/freedoms-fortress-deactivated-after-188-years-of-service/.

Joshi, Sonalee A., Elizabeth R. Duval, Bradley Kubat, and Israel Liberzon. "A Review of Hippocampal Activation in Post-traumatic Stress Disorder." *Psychophysiology* 57, no. 1 (January 2020). https://doi.org/10.1111/psyp.13357.

Konvisser, Z. "From Terror to Meaning and Healing – A Franklian View." *The International Forum for Logotherapy*, 2016.

LaCasse, Matthew. "Rewriting the Narrative With Logotherapy: Review of Man's Search for Meaning." *American Journal of Psychiatry Residents' Journal* 12, no. 7 (July 2017): 12. https://doi.org/10.1176/appi.ajp-rj.2017.120707.

LivingWorks. "ASIST Suicide Prevention Training Program." Accessed May 16, 2019. https://www.livingworks.net/asist.

Lochan, Radha and Helen Heacock. "How Do You Sleep at Night?: A Survey Study on Sleep Deprivation and Cognition." *BCIT Environmental Public Health Journal*, August 8, 2014. https://doi.org/10.47339/ephj.2014.152.

Lofgren, Stephen J., ed. *Then Came the Fire: Personal Accounts from the Pentagon, 11 September 2001*. Washington, DC: Center of Military History, United States Army, 2011.

Lowell, A., B. Suarez-Jimenez, L. Helpman, X. Zhu, A. Durosky, A. Hilburn, F. Schneier, R. Gross, and Y. Neria. "9/11-Related PTSD among Highly Exposed Populations: A Systematic Review 15 Years after the Attack." *Psychological Medicine* 48, no. 4 (March 2018): 537–53. https://doi.org/10.1017/S0033291717002033.

"LTG Timothy J. Maude, USA – 9/11 Pentagon Memorial." Accessed April 29, 2020. https://pentagonmemorial.org/biographies/ltg-timothy-j-maude-usa/.

Luft, B. J., C. Schechter, R. Kotov, J. Broihier, D. Reissman, K. Guerrera, I. Udasin, J. Moline, D. Harrison, G. Friedman-Jimenez, R. H. Pietrzak, S. M. Southwick, and E. J. Bromet. "Exposure, Probable PTSD and Lower Respiratory Illness among World Trade Center Rescue, Recovery and Clean-up Workers." *Psychological Medicine* 42, no. 5 (May 2012): 1069–79. https://doi.org/10.1017/S003329171100256X.

Maddox, Stephanie A., Jakob Hartmann, Rachel A. Ross, and Kerry J. Ressler. "Deconstructing the Gestalt: Mechanisms of Fear, Threat, and Trauma Memory Encoding." *Neuron* 102, no. 1 (April 2019): 60–74. https://doi.org/10.1016/j.neuron.2019.03.017.

Maslow, Carey B., Kimberly Caramanica, Alice E. Welch, Steven D. Stellman, Robert M. Brackbill, and Mark R. Farfel. "Trajectories of Scores on a Screening Instrument for PTSD Among World Trade Center Rescue, Recovery, and Clean-Up Workers: Trajectories of PTSD in 9/11 Responders." *Journal of Traumatic Stress* 28, no. 3 (June 2015): 198–205. https://doi.org/10.1002/jts.22011.

McDonnell, Janet. *The National Park Service Responding to the September 11 Terrorist Attacks*, 2013.

Mental Health Policy, Plans and Programmes: Updated Version. Rev. ed. Mental Health Policy and Service Guidance Package, 2,1. Geneva: World Health Organization, 2005.

Morris, David J. *The Evil Hours: A Biography of Post-Traumatic Stress Disorder*. Boston: Houghton Mifflin Harcourt, 2015.

Morris, Lydia and Warren Mansell. "A Systematic Review of the Relationship between Rigidity/Flexibility and Transdiagnostic Cognitive and Behavioral Processes That Maintain Psychopathology." *Journal of Experimental Psychopathology* 9, no. 3 (July 1, 2018). https://doi.org/10.1177/2043808718779431.

Murray, Hannah, Yasmin Pethania, and Evelina Medin. "Survivor Guilt: A Cognitive Approach." *The Cognitive Behaviour Therapist* 14 (2021): e28. https://doi.org/10.1017/S1754470X21000246.

Myers, Diane Garaventa and David F. Wee. *Disaster Mental Health Services: A Primer for Practitioners*. Brunner-Routledge Psychosocial Stress Series 27. New York: Brunner-Routledge, 2005.

National Center for PTSD. "PTSD: National Center for PTSD Home." 2022. https://www.ptsd.va.gov/index.asp.

National Commission on Terrorist Attacks upon the United States, Thomas H. Kean, and Lee Hamilton, eds. *The 9/11 Commission Report: Final Report of the National Commission on Terrorist Attacks upon the United States*. Official government ed. Washington, DC: National Commission on Terrorist Attacks upon the United States.

National Guard. "ARNG Soldier Avoids Pentagon Attack by Chance Visit to Son at Day Care Center." Accessed December 20, 2020. https://www.nationalguard.mil/News/Article-View/Article/573566/arng-soldier-avoids-pentagon-attack-by-chance-visit-to-son-at-day-care-center/.

National Parks Conservation Association. "Flight 93." Accessed November 5, 2019. https://www.npca.org/parks/flight-93-national-memorial.

National Response Team. "Observations and Lessons Learned from the World Trade Center and Pentagon Terrorist Attacks." Accessed October 24, 2019. https://exhibit.apus.edu/items/show/1517.

Naveed, Riaz, Malik Sadie, and Nawaz Sehrish. "Well-Being and Post-Traumatic Stress Disorder Due to Natural and Man-Made Disasters on Adults." *Pakistan Journal of Medical Research* 54, no. 1 (March 2015): 25–28.

Nelson, Alex. "Pentagon 9/11 Attack: What Happened, What Year Was It, What Time Did Flight 77 Crash, How Many People Died?" National World, August 30, 2022. https://www.nationalworld.com/news/world/pentagon-911-attack-what-time-did-flight-77-crash-what-is-the-building-used-for-and-how-many-people-died-3372416.

Neria, Yuval, Laura DiGrande, and Ben G. Adams. "Posttraumatic Stress Disorder Following the September 11, 2001, Terrorist Attacks: A Review of the Literature among Highly Exposed Populations." *American Psychologist* 66, no. 6 (2011): 429–46. https://doi.org/10.1037/a0024791.

New York Daily News. "PTSD, Survivor's Guilt, and the Hidden Emotional Toll Caused by Mass Shootings." Accessed May 1, 2019. https://www.nydailynews.com/news/national/ny-guilt-tragic-effects-mass-shootings-20190325-qz5uhx2zhja4nm4spt2honvqtq-story.html.

Non-Standard Employment around the World: Understanding Challenges, Shaping Prospects. Geneva: International Labour Office, 2016.

"Norma Cruz Khan – 9/11 Pentagon Memorial." Accessed February 2, 2019. https://pentagonmemorial.org/biographies/norma-cruz-khan/.

"Official Website of the Joint Chiefs of Staff." Accessed November 29, 2021. https://www.jcs.mil/.

Parker, Gordon. "In Search of Logotherapy." *Australian & New Zealand Journal of Psychiatry* 56, no. 7 (July 2022): 742–44. https://doi.org/10.1177/00048674211062830.

PBS NewsHour. "Flight Data and Voice Recorders Found At Pentagon." September 14, 2001. https://www.pbs.org/newshour/world/terrorism-july-dec01-washington_09-14.

Perrin, Megan A., Laura DiGrande, Katherine Wheeler, Lorna Thorpe, Mark Farfel, and Robert Brackbill. "Differences in PTSD Prevalence and Associated Risk Factors Among World Trade Center Disaster Rescue and Recovery Workers." *American Journal of Psychiatry* 164, no. 9 (September 2007): 1385–94. https://doi.org/10.1176/appi.ajp.2007.06101645.

"Reston Mourns Its Losses." Accessed February 2, 2019. http://www.connectionnewspapers.com/news/2006/sep/05/reston-mourns-its-losses/.

Rigutto, Claudia, Adegboyega O. Sapara, and Vincent I. O. Agyapong. "Anxiety, Depression and Posttraumatic Stress Disorder after Terrorist Attacks: A General Review of the Literature." *Behavioral Sciences* 11, no. 10 (October 19, 2021): 140. https://doi.org/10.3390/bs11100140.

Roos, Dave. "How the Pentagon's Design Saved Lives on September 11." HISTORY, September 11, 2019. https://www.history.com/news/pentagon-design-september-11-attacks.

Ross, Colin A. "Self-Blame and Suicidal Ideation Among Combat Veterans." *American Journal of Psychotherapy* 67, no. 4 (October 2013): 309–22. https://doi.org/10.1176/appi.psychotherapy.2013.67.4.309.

Rossow, Robert, and Office of the Deputy Chief of Staff, Department of the Army. *Uncommon Strength: The Story of the Office of the Army Deputy Chief of Staff for Personnel during the Attack on the Pentagon, 11 September 2001*, 2003.

"RUDAW." Accessed March 20, 2022. https://www.rudaw.net/english.

SAVE. "SAVE: Suicide Prevention, Information, and Awareness." Accessed November 29, 2020. https://save.org/.

Schiraldi, Glenn R. *The Post-Traumatic Stress Disorder Sourcebook: A Guide to Healing, Recovery, and Growth*. 2nd ed. New York, [N.Y.]: McGraw-Hill, 2009.

Schulenberg, Stefan E., Robert R. Hutzell, Carrie Nassif, and Julius M. Rogina. "Logotherapy for Clinical Practice." *Psychotherapy: Theory, Research, Practice, Training* 45, no. 4 (2008): 447–63. https://doi.org/10.1037/a0014331.

Schwartz, James. "The Critical Role of First Responders: Sharing Lessons Learned from Past Attacks." *Hearing Before the Committee on Homeland Security, House of Representatives, One Hundred Thirteenth Congress, Second Session*, June 18, 2014. https://www.iafc.org/docs/default-source/uploaded-documents/grTestimonySchwartzHomeSec140618.pdf.

Selva, Joaquin. "Master Resilience Training (MRT) in the US Army: PowerPoint & Interview." *PositivePsychology.com*, November 28, 2017. https://positivepsychology.com/master-resilience-training-mrt/.

Sharps, Matthew Joseph. *Processing under Pressure: Stress, Memory, and Decision-Making in Law Enforcement*. Third edition. Flushing, NY: Looseleaf Law Publications, Inc, 2022.

Smith, Erin C., Lisa Holmes, and Frederick M. Burkle. "The Physical and Mental Health Challenges Experienced by 9/11 First Responders and Recovery Workers: A Review of the Literature." *Prehospital and Disaster Medicine* 34, no. 6 (December 2019): 625–31. https://doi.org/10.1017/S1049023X19004989.

"Soldier's Medal," n.d. https://military-history.fandom.com/wiki/Soldier%27s_Medal.

Southwick, Steven M., Robin Gilmartin, Patrick McDonough, and Paul Morrissey. "Logotherapy as an Adjunctive Treatment for Chronic Combat-Related PTSD: A Meaning-Based Intervention." *American Journal of Psychotherapy* 60, no. 2 (April 2006): 161–74. https://doi.org/10.1176/appi.psychotherapy.2006.60.2.161.

Stellman, Jeanne Mager, Rebecca P. Smith, Craig L. Katz, Vansh Sharma, Dennis S. Charney, Robin Herbert, Jacqueline Moline, Benjamin J. Luft, Steven Markowitz, Iris Udasin, Denise Harrison, Sherry Baron, Philip J. Landrigan, Stephen M. Levin, and Steven Southwick. "Enduring Mental Health Morbidity and Social Function Impairment in World Trade Center Rescue, Recovery, and Cleanup Workers: The Psychological Dimension of an Environmental Health Disaster." *Environmental Health Perspectives* 116, no. 9 (September 2008): 1248–53. https://doi.org/10.1289/ehp.11164.

"Supplemental Material for Factors Predicting the Development of Psychopathology Among First Responders: A Prospective, Longitudinal Study." *Psychological Trauma: Theory, Research, Practice, and Policy*, 2021, tra0000957.supp. https://doi.org/10.1037/tra0000957.supp.

"Survivors and Supporters Rally to Prevent Suicide on Capitol Hill | TAPS." Accessed June 29, 2022. https://www.taps.org/articles/2019/prevent-suicide-rally.

Sutton, Jeremy. "Socratic Questioning in Psychology: Examples and Techniques." *PositivePsychology.com*, June 19, 2020. https://positivepsychology.com/socratic-questioning/.

Tate, Kevin A., Cyrus Williams, and Dia Harden. "Finding Purpose in Pain: Using Logotherapy as a Method for Addressing Survivor Guilt in First-Generation College Students." *Journal of College Counseling* 16, no. 1 (April 2013): 79–92. https://doi.org/10.1002/j.2161-1882.2013.00028.x.

"The Chesapeake Bay Impact Crater." Accessed November 21, 2020. https://www.ndsu.edu/pubweb/~ashworth/webpages/g491/2002presentations/rhondaolson/webpage.htm#:~:text=Approximately%2035%20million%20years%20ago,to%20be%201.3km%20deep.

The Virginian-Pilot. "Norfolk Marine, 75 Years | Anniversary Issue." Accessed June 4, 2019. https://www.pilotonline.com/inside-business/special-reports/vp-ib-ai-norfolk-marine-0712-20210712-avow4cg4onafzbeve6c5fmn6r4-story.html.

Titan Systems Corporation. "Arlington County After-Action Report on the Response to the September 11 Terrorist Attack on the Pentagon." 2003. https://www.policinginstitute.org/wp-content/uploads/2018/07/pentagonafteractionreport.pdf.

"Tragedy Assistance Program For Survivors (TAPS) Is Here For You!" Accessed April 4, 2021. https://www.taps.org/.

Tyng, Chai M., Hafeez U. Amin, Mohamad N. M. Saad, and Aamir S. Malik. "The Influences of Emotion on Learning and Memory." *Frontiers in Psychology* 8 (August 24, 2017): Article 1454. https://doi.org/10.3389/fpsyg.2017.01454.

"Veteran Trash Talk." Accessed November 29, 2021. https://veterantrashtalk.com/.

Virginia Guard Public Affairs. *Virginia Guardsman Awarded Soldier's Medal for Heroism.* July 23, 2010. Photo. https://www.flickr.com/photos/vaguardpao/4822421552/.

Whalen, Ronald. "In Defense of After-Action Reviews: The Art and Science of Small Unit Coping." *Military Review*, April 2010.

Wright, Lawrence. *The Looming Tower: Al-Qaeda and the Road to 9/11.* New York: Knopf, 2006.

ENDNOTES

1 For Flight 77 path and deaths details, see:

Alex Nelson, "Pentagon 9/11 Attack: What Happened, What Year Was It, What Time Did Flight 77 Crash, How Many People Died?" National World, August 30, 2022, https://www.nationalworld.com/news/world/pentagon-911-attack-what-time-did-flight-77-crash-what-is-the-building-used-for-and-how-many-people-died-3372416.

Patricia Bauer, "American Airlines Flight 77 | Facts & History | Britannica," September 4, 2022, https://www.britannica.com/event/American-Airlines-flight-77.

2 For reports evaluating the incident response and a view of the response on the ground, see:

National Response Team, "Observations and Lessons Learned from the World Trade Center and Pentagon Terrorist Attacks," Accessed October 24, 2019, https://exhibit.apus.edu/items/show/1517.

Janet McDonnell, *The National Park Service Responding to the September 11 Terrorist Attacks*, 2013.

3 Sources for Pentagon attack information included in-person interviews of those in the acknowledgment pages, as well as interviews of those that did not want their name to be a part of this book. Other references include the following books and website references:

Dave Roos, "How the Pentagon's Design Saved Lives on September 11," HISTORY, September 11, 2019, https://www.history.com/news/pentagon-design-september-11-attacks.

Patrick Creed and Rick Newman, *Firefight: Inside the Battle to Save the Pentagon on 9/11*, New York: Presidio Press/Ballantine

Books, 2008.

Alfred Goldberg, Sarandis Papadopoulos, Diane Putney, Nancy Berlage, and Rebecca Welch, *Pentagon 9/11,* Defense Studies Series, Washington, DC: Historical Office, Office of the Secretary of Defense, 2007.

Stephen J. Lofgren, ed., *Then Came the Fire: Personal Accounts from the Pentagon, 11 September 2001,* Washington, DC: Center of Military History, United States Army, 2011.

Robert Rossow and Office of the Deputy Chief of Staff, Department of the Army, *Uncommon Strength: The Story of the Office of the Army Deputy Chief of Staff for Personnel during the Attack on the Pentagon, 11 September 2001,* 2003.

4   For an in-depth historical review of the 9/11 attack on the Pentagon by the Office of the Secretary of Defense Historical Office, please read the "Pentagon 9/11."

Goldberg, Papadopoulos, Putney, Berlage, and Welch, *Pentagon 9/11.*

5   "LTG Timothy J. Maude, USA – 9/11 Pentagon Memorial," accessed April 29, 2020, https://pentagonmemorial.org/biographies/ltg-timothy-j-maude-usa/.

Goldberg, Papadopoulos, Putney, Berlage, and Welch, *Pentagon 9/11*, 36.

6   Goldberg, Papadopoulos, Putney, Berlage, and Welch, *Pentagon 9/11*, 30.

7   The weight of the Flight 77 plane was 180,000 pounds, or 90 tons. Source:

Goldberg, Papadopoulos, Putney, Berlage, and Welch, *Pentagon 9/11.*

8   The US Army's Resource Services-Washington's Program and Budget

Division, lost 25 of its 28 employees, with the other three sustaining injuries as well. Source:

Goldberg, Papadopoulos, Putney, Berlage, and Welch, *Pentagon 9/11*, 26.

9 For details on Arlington County's response to the Pentagon on 9/11, see Arlington County—After-Action Report on the Response to the September 11 Terrorist Attack on the Pentagon: Titan Systems Corporation, "Arlington County After-Action Report on the Response to the September 11 Terrorist Attack on the Pentagon," 2003, https://www.policinginstitute.org/wp-content/uploads/2018/07/pentagonafteractionreport.pdf.

10 For additional information on the creation of the MMRS, please see these references:

Intelligence Resource Program, "1999 Congressional Hearings," *Federation of American Scientists*, 2000, https://irp.fas.org/congress/1999_hr/index.html.

James Schwartz, "The Critical Role of First Responders: Sharing Lessons Learned from Past Attacks," *Hearing Before the Committee on Homeland Security, House of Representatives, One Hundred Thirteenth Congress, Second Session*, June 18, 2014, https://www.iafc.org/docs/default-source/uploaded-documents/grTestimonySchwartzHomeSec140618.pdf.

11 Arlington County Lessons Learned Report:

"Arlington County Conference Report," Arlington, VA, 2003, https://arlingtonva.s3.amazonaws.com/wp-content/uploads/sites/21/2014/04/2012-ARCO_Conf_Report.pdf.

12 Titan Systems Corporation, "Arlington County AAR."

13 "Official Website of the Joint Chiefs of Staff," accessed November 29, 2021, https://www.jcs.mil/.

14   For detailed accounts of the history of al Qaeda, please see the following references:

Lawrence Wright, *The Looming Tower: Al-Qaeda and the Road to 9/11,* New York: Knopf, 2006.

National Commission on Terrorist Attacks upon the United States, Thomas H. Kean, and Lee Hamilton, eds, *The 9/11 Commission Report: Final Report of the National Commission on Terrorist Attacks upon the United States,* Official government ed., Washington, DC: National Commission on Terrorist Attacks upon the United States.

15   Federal Bureau of Investigation, "World Trade Center Bombing 1993," accessed November 29, 2021, https://www.fbi.gov/history/famous-cases/world-trade-center-bombing-1993.

History.com Editors, "World Trade Center Is Bombed," *HISTORY,* accessed August 28, 2019, https://www.history.com/this-day-in-history/world-trade-center-bombed.

"Foreign Terrorists in America," accessed June 29, 2020, https://irp.fas.org/congress/1998_hr/s980224c.htm.

16   History.com Editors, "World Trade Center Bombed."

ICC, "Today in History: World Trade Center Is Bombed," accessed November 29, 2020, https://www.iccsafe.org/building-safety-journal/bsj-dives/today-in-history-world-trade-center-is-bombed/.

17   PBS NewsHour, "Flight Data and Voice Recorders Found At Pentagon," September 14, 2001, https://www.pbs.org/newshour/world/terrorism-july-dec01-washington_09-14.

18   "Norma Cruz Khan – 9/11 Pentagon Memorial," accessed February 2, 2019, https://pentagonmemorial.org/biographies/norma-cruz-khan/.

"Reston Mourns Its Losses," accessed February 2, 2019, http://www.connectionnewspapers.com/news/2006/sep/05/reston-mourns-its-losses/.

19 National Parks Conservation Association, "Flight 93," accessed November 5, 2019, https://www.npca.org/parks/flight-93-national-al-memorial.

20 Rossow and Office of the Deputy Chief of Staff, Department of the Army, *Uncommon Strength,* 2.

21 National Guard, "ARNG Soldier Avoids Pentagon Attack by Chance Visit to Son at Day Care Center," accessed December 20, 2020. https://www.nationalguard.mil/News/Article-View/Article/573566/arng-soldier-avoids-pentagon-attack-by-chance-visit-to-son-at-day-care-center/.

22 New York Daily News, "PTSD, Survivor's Guilt, and the Hidden Emotional Toll Caused by Mass Shootings," accessed May 1, 2019, https://www.nydailynews.com/news/national/ny-guilt-tragic-effects-mass-shootings-20190325-qz5uhx2zhja4nm4spt2honvqtq-story.html.

23 Recommended readings about survivor guilt include:
    Colin A. Ross, "Self-Blame and Suicidal Ideation Among Combat Veterans," *American Journal of Psychotherapy* 67, no. 4 (October 2013): 309–22, https://doi.org/10.1176/appi.psychotherapy.2013.67.4.309.
    Hannah Murray, Yasmin Pethania, and Evelina Medin, "Survivor Guilt: A Cognitive Approach," *The Cognitive Behaviour Therapist* 14 (2021): e28, https://doi.org/10.1017/S1754470X21000246.
    Ramona Fimiani, Francesco Gazzillo, Nino Dazzi, and Marshall Bush, "Survivor Guilt: Theoretical, Empirical, and Clinical Features," *International Forum of Psychoanalysis* 31, no. 3 (July 3, 2022): 176–90, https://doi.org/10.1080/0803706X.2021.1941246.

24 Thomas Joiner of Florida State University developed the Interpersonal-Psychological Theory of Suicidal Behavior. Joiner postulates that a suicidal person feels that he or she does not belong and that

they are a burden to others. Those feelings, along with the acquired capability for suicide, are the perfect storm leading to a completed suicide. See this reference for more:

Thomas E. Joiner, *Why People Die by Suicide,* Cambridge, Mass: Harvard University Press, 2005.

25 Diane Garaventa Myers and David F. Wee, *Disaster Mental Health Services: A Primer for Practitioners,* Brunner-Routledge Psychosocial Stress Series 27, New York: Brunner-Routledge, 2005.

26 Kevin A. Tate, Cyrus Williams, and Dia Harden, "Finding Purpose in Pain: Using Logotherapy as a Method for Addressing Survivor Guilt in First-Generation College Students," *Journal of College Counseling* 16, no. 1 (April 2013): 79–92, https://doi.org/10.1002/j.2161-1882.2013.00028.x.

Kallio Hunnicutt-Ferguson, Katarzyna E. Wyka, Melissa Peskin, Judith Cukor, Megan Olden, and JoAnn Difede, "Posttraumatic Stress Disorder, Functional Impairment, and Subjective Distress in World Trade Center Disaster Workers: PTSD and Impairment in Disaster Workers," *Journal of Traumatic Stress* 31, no. 2 (April 2018): 234–43, https://doi.org/10.1002/jts.22268.

Judith Cukor, Katarzyna Wyka, Brittany Mello, Megan Olden, Nimali Jayasinghe, Jennifer Roberts, Cezar Giosan, Michael Crane, and JoAnn Difede, "The Longitudinal Course of PTSD among Disaster Workers Deployed to the World Trade Center Following the Attacks of September 11th," *Journal of Traumatic Stress* 24, no. 5 (October 2011): 506–14, https://doi.org/10.1002/jts.20672.

27 Tate, Williams, and Harden, "Finding Purpose in Pain."

28 Holocaust survivor Viktor Frankl developed a psychotherapy or counseling method called "logotherapy." In his 1946 book, *Man's Search for Meaning,* he lays out his philosophy and psychothera-peutic technique that he conceived as a prisoner of war in a Nazi

concentration camp during World War II. Frankl talks of his life as a prisoner of war, and then writes about how he found meaning in every ephemeral flash of time of his life in the concentration camp. Frankl was able to avoid fatalistic thinking, a thinking defined by helplessness and having no control over what happens. He found a way to hold onto the belief that he was in charge of his future in that he could choose to keep hope of a future alive instead of giving up hope and submitting to his captors. When that hope was gone, the future was gone, and life would then have no meaning.

Viktor E. Frankl, William J. Winslade, and Harold S. Kushner, *Man's Search for Meaning,* Translated by Helen Pisano and Ilse Lasch, Boston, Mass.: Beacon Press, 2015.

29   Publications about Viktor Frankl's logotherapy technique include the following:

Stefan E. Schulenberg, Robert R. Hutzell, Carrie Nassif, and Julius M. Rogina, "Logotherapy for Clinical Practice," *Psychotherapy: Theory, Research, Practice, Training* 45, no. 4 (2008): 447–63, https://doi.org/10.1037/a0014331.

Gordon Parker, "In Search of Logotherapy," *Australian & New Zealand Journal of Psychiatry* 56, no. 7 (July 2022): 742–44, https://doi.org/10.1177/00048674211062830.

W. Thomas Baumel and John N. Constantino, "Implementing Logotherapy in Its Second Half-Century: Incorporating Existential Considerations Into Personalized Treatment of Adolescent Depression," *Journal of the American Academy of Child & Adolescent Psychiatry* 59, no. 9 (September 2020): 1012–15, https://doi.org/10.1016/j.jaac.2020.06.006.

Tate, Williams, and Harden, "Finding Purpose in Pain."

Matthew LaCasse, "Rewriting the Narrative With Logotherapy: Review of Man's Search for Meaning," *American Journal of Psychiatry Residents' Journal* 12, no. 7 (July 2017): 12, https://doi.org/10.1176/appi.ajp-rj.2017.120707.

Z. Konvisser, "From Terror to Meaning and Healing – A Franklian View," *The International Forum for Logotherapy*, 2016.

30   Jeremy Sutton, "Socratic Questioning in Psychology: Examples and Techniques," *PositivePsychology.com*, June 19, 2020, https://positivepsychology.com/socratic-questioning/.

31   Steven M. Southwick, Robin Gilmartin, Patrick McDonough, and Paul Morrissey, "Logotherapy as an Adjunctive Treatment for Chronic Combat-Related PTSD: A Meaning-Based Intervention," *American Journal of Psychotherapy* 60, no. 2 (April 2006): 161–74, https://doi.org/10.1176/appi.psychotherapy.2006.60.2.161.
R. Gilmartin and S. Southwick, "Combat-Related PTSD and Logotherapy," *International Forum for Logotherapy*, 2004.

32   The American Psychiatric Association (APA) publishes the authoritative guide for mental health professionals to diagnose mental disorders, the Diagnostic and Statistical Manual of Mental Disorders (DSM).
American Psychiatric Association, *Diagnostic and Statistical Manual of Mental Disorders*, 5th ed., American Psychiatric Association, 2013, https://doi.org/10.1176/appi.books.9780890425596.

33   For a good read that covers apophenia and PTSD, look for David Morris' book, *The Evil Hours*.
David J. Morris, *The Evil Hours: A Biography of Post-Traumatic Stress Disorder,* Boston: Houghton Mifflin Harcourt, 2015.

34   Claudia Rigutto, Adegboyega O. Sapara, and Vincent I. O. Agyapong, "Anxiety, Depression and Posttraumatic Stress Disorder after Terrorist Attacks: A General Review of the Literature," *Behavioral Sciences* 11, no. 10 (October 19, 2021): 140, https://doi.org/10.3390/bs11100140.

35   Erin C. Smith, Lisa Holmes, and Frederick M. Burkle, "The Physical and Mental Health Challenges Experienced by 9/11 First Responders

and Recovery Workers: A Review of the Literature," *Prehospital and Disaster Medicine* 34, no. 6 (December 2019): 625–31, https://doi.org/10.1017/S1049023X19004989.

36   American Psychiatric Association, *DSM-V.*

37   American Psychiatric Association, *Diagnostic and Statistical Manual of Mental Disorders*, 4th ed., 1994.

38   American Psychiatric Association, *DSM-V.*

39   Rigutto, Sapara, and Agyapong, "Anxiety, Depression and Posttraumatic Stress Disorder after Terrorist Attacks."

Mira Brancu, Monica Mann-Wrobel, Jean C. Beckham, H. Ryan Wagner, Alyssa Elliott, Allison T. Robbins, Madrianne Wong, Ania E. Berchuck, and Jennifer J. Runnals, "Subthreshold Posttraumatic Stress Disorder: A Meta-Analytic Review of DSM-IV Prevalence and a Proposed DSM-5 Approach to Measurement," *Psychological Trauma: Theory, Research, Practice and Policy* 8, no. 2 (March 2016): 222–32, https://doi.org/10.1037/tra0000078.

Yuval Neria, Laura DiGrande, and Ben G. Adams, "Posttraumatic Stress Disorder Following the September 11, 2001, Terrorist Attacks: A Review of the Literature among Highly Exposed Populations," *American Psychologist* 66, no. 6 (2011): 429–46, https://doi.org/10.1037/a0024791.

40   Glenn R. Schiraldi, *The Post-Traumatic Stress Disorder Sourcebook: A Guide to Healing, Recovery, and Growth,* 2nd ed., New York, [N.Y.]: McGraw-Hill, 2009.

Charles R. Figley, ed., *Brief Treatments for the Traumatized: A Project of the Green Cross Foundation,* Contributions in Psychology, no. 39, Westport, Conn: Greenwood Press, 2002.

41   Riaz Naveed, Malik Sadie, and Nawaz Sehrish, "Well-Being and Post-Traumatic Stress Disorder Due to Natural and Man-Made

Disasters on Adults," *Pakistan Journal of Medical Research* 54, no. 1 (March 2015): 25–28.

42   Jeanne Mager Stellman, Rebecca P. Smith, Craig L. Katz, Vansh Sharma, Dennis S. Charney, Robin Herbert, Jacqueline Moline, Benjamin J. Luft, Steven Markowitz, Iris Udasin, Denise Harrison, Sherry Baron, Philip J. Landrigan, Stephen M. Levin, and Steven Southwick, "Enduring Mental Health Morbidity and Social Function Impairment in World Trade Center Rescue, Recovery, and Cleanup Workers: The Psychological Dimension of an Environmental Health Disaster," *Environmental Health Perspectives* 116, no. 9 (September 2008): 1248–53, https://doi.org/10.1289/ehp.11164.

B. J. Luft, C. Schechter, R. Kotov, J. Broihier, D. Reissman, K. Guerrera, I. Udasin, J. Moline, D. Harrison, G. Friedman-Jimenez, R. H. Pietrzak, S. M. Southwick, and E. J. Bromet, "Exposure, Probable PTSD and Lower Respiratory Illness among World Trade Center Rescue, Recovery and Clean-up Workers," *Psychological Medicine* 42, no. 5 (May 2012): 1069–79, https://doi.org/10.1017/S003329171100256X.

43   Smith, Holmes, and Burkle, "Physical and Mental Health Challenges Experienced by 9/11 First Responders and Recovery Workers."

44   Carey B. Maslow, Kimberly Caramanica, Alice E. Welch, Steven D. Stellman, Robert M. Brackbill, and Mark R. Farfel, "Trajectories of Scores on a Screening Instrument for PTSD Among World Trade Center Rescue, Recovery, and Clean-Up Workers: Trajectories of PTSD in 9/11 Responders," *Journal of Traumatic Stress* 28, no. 3 (June 2015): 198–205, https://doi.org/10.1002/jts.22011.

45   Rigutto, Sapara, and Agyapong, "Anxiety, Depression and Posttraumatic Stress Disorder after Terrorist Attacks."

46   Neria, DiGrande, and Adams, "PTSD Following the September 11,

2001, Terrorist Attacks."

47   Rigutto, Sapara, and Agyapong, "Anxiety, Depression and Posttraumatic Stress Disorder after Terrorist Attacks."

Hunnicutt-Ferguson, Wyka, Peskin, Cukor, Olden, and Difede, "PTSD and Impairment in Disaster Workers."

A. Lowell, B. Suarez-Jimenez, L. Helpman, X. Zhu, A. Durosky, A. Hilburn, F. Schneier, R. Gross, and Y. Neria, "9/11-Related PTSD among Highly Exposed Populations: A Systematic Review 15 Years after the Attack," *Psychological Medicine* 48, no. 4 (March 2018): 537–53, https://doi.org/10.1017/S0033291717002033.

48   Among responders in the WTC Health Registry, the rate of probable PTSD was three times higher in unaffiliated volunteers (21.2%) than in police (6.2%). Source:

Megan A. Perrin, Laura DiGrande, Katherine Wheeler, Lorna Thorpe, Mark Farfel, and Robert Brackbill, "Differences in PTSD Prevalence and Associated Risk Factors Among World Trade Center Disaster Rescue and Recovery Workers," *American Journal of Psychiatry* 164, no. 9 (September 2007): 1385–94, https://doi.org/10.1176/appi.ajp.2007.06101645.

49   Luft, Schechter, Kotov, Broihier, Reissman, Guerrera, Udasin, Moline, Harrison, Friedman-Jimenez, Pietrzak, Southwick, and Bromet, "PTSD and Respiratory Illness among WTC Rescue, Recovery and Clean-up Workers."

50   Neria, DiGrande, and Adams, "PTSD Following the September 11, 2001, Terrorist Attacks."

51   The Department of Veterans Affairs has a National Center for PTSD with information and resources for veterans.

National Center for PTSD, "PTSD: National Center for PTSD Home," 2022. https://www.ptsd.va.gov/index.asp.

52   Robyn L. Hacker and John J. Horan, "Policing People with Mental Illness: Experimental Evaluation of Online Training to de-Escalate Mental Health Crises," *Journal of Experimental Criminology* 15, no. 4 (December 2019): 551–67, https://doi.org/10.1007/s11292-019-09380-3.

Michele P. Bratina, Kelly M. Carrero, Bitna Kim, and Alida V. Merlo, "Crisis Intervention Team Training: When Police Encounter Persons with Mental Illness," *Police Practice and Research* 21, no. 3 (May 3, 2020): 279–96, https://doi.org/10.1080/15614263.2018.1484290.

Michele P. Bratina, Jacqueline A. Carsello, Kelly M. Carrero, and Michael E. Antonio, "An Examination of Crisis Intervention Teams in Rural Jurisdictions," *Community Mental Health Journal* 57, no. 7 (October 2021): 1388–98, https://doi.org/10.1007/s10597-021-00797-7.

Horace A. Ellis, "Effects of a Crisis Intervention Team (CIT) Training Program Upon Police Officers Before and After Crisis Intervention Team Training," *Archives of Psychiatric Nursing* 28, no. 1 (February 2014): 10–16, https://doi.org/10.1016/j.apnu.2013.10.003.

53   Chris Giacomantonio, Stephanie Goodwin, and Garland Carmichael, "Learning to De-Escalate: Evaluating the Behavioural Impact of Verbal Judo Training on Police Constables," *Police Practice and Research* 21, no. 4 (July 3, 2020): 401–17, https://doi.org/10.1080/15614263.2019.1589472.

54   For information about the impact of emotions on learning and memory, please see the following references:

Chai M. Tyng, Hafeez U. Amin, Mohamad N. M. Saad, and Aamir S. Malik, "The Influences of Emotion on Learning and Memory," *Frontiers in Psychology* 8 (August 24, 2017): Article 1454, https://doi.org/10.3389/fpsyg.2017.01454.

Graham Davies, "Book Review: Handbook of Eyewitness

Psychology. Volume 1. Memory for Events," *Applied Cognitive Psychology* 21, no. 8 (December 2007): 1113–14, https://doi.org/10.1002/acp.1397.

55   For research regarding PTSD encoding and brain operations, please refer to the following publications:

Stephanie A. Maddox, Jakob Hartmann, Rachel A. Ross, and Kerry J. Ressler, "Deconstructing the Gestalt: Mechanisms of Fear, Threat, and Trauma Memory Encoding," *Neuron* 102, no. 1 (April 2019): 60–74, https://doi.org/10.1016/j.neuron.2019.03.017.

Michele Garibbo, Jessica Aylward, and Oliver J Robinson, "The Impact of Threat of Shock-Induced Anxiety on the Neural Substrates of Memory Encoding and Retrieval," *Social Cognitive and Affective Neuroscience* 14, no. 10 (October 1, 2019): 1087–96, https://doi.org/10.1093/scan/nsz080.

Sorcha Bolton and Oliver J. Robinson, "The Impact of Threat of Shock-Induced Anxiety on Memory Encoding and Retrieval," *Learning & Memory* 24, no. 10 (October 2017): 532–42, https://doi.org/10.1101/lm.045187.117.

Sonalee A. Joshi, Elizabeth R. Duval, Bradley Kubat, and Israel Liberzon, "A Review of Hippocampal Activation in Post-traumatic Stress Disorder," *Psychophysiology* 57, no. 1 (January 2020), https://doi.org/10.1111/psyp.13357.

56   For more information about the importance of sleep and its relation to the brain and behavior, please see the following references:

Maryann C. Deak and Robert Stickgold, "Sleep and Cognition," *WIREs Cognitive Science* 1, no. 4 (July 2010): 491–500, https://doi.org/10.1002/wcs.52.

Radha Lochan and Helen Heacock, "How Do You Sleep at Night?: A Survey Study on Sleep Deprivation and Cognition," *BCIT Environmental Public Health Journal*, August 8, 2014, https://doi.org/10.47339/ephj.2014.152.

Jessica R. Dietch, Camilo J. Ruggero, Keke Schuler, Daniel J. Taylor, Benjamin J. Luft, and Roman Kotov, "Posttraumatic Stress Disorder Symptoms and Sleep in the Daily Lives of World Trade Center Responders," *Journal of Occupational Health Psychology* 24, no. 6 (December 2019): 689–702, https://doi.org/10.1037/ocp0000158.

57   Garry Huang, Tso-Ying Lee, Kondwani Joseph Banda, Li-Chung Pien, Hsiu-Ju Jen, Ruey Chen, Doresses Liu, Shu-Tai Shen Hsiao, and Kuei-Ru Chou, "Prevalence of Sleep Disorders among First Responders for Medical Emergencies: A Meta-Analysis," *Journal of Global Health* 12 (October 20, 2022): 04092, https://doi.org/10.7189/jogh.12.04092.

Talya R. Feldman, Caryn L. Carlson, Leslie K. Rice, Marc I. Kruse, Christopher G. Beevers, Michael J. Telch, and Robert A. Josephs, "Factors Predicting the Development of Psychopathology among First Responders: A Prospective, Longitudinal Study," *Psychological Trauma: Theory, Research, Practice, and Policy* 13, no. 1 (January 2021): 75–83, https://doi.org/10.1037/tra0000957.

"Supplemental Material for Factors Predicting the Development of Psychopathology Among First Responders: A Prospective, Longitudinal Study," *Psychological Trauma: Theory, Research, Practice, and Policy*, 2021, tra0000957.supp. https://doi.org/10.1037/tra0000957.supp.

58   Mark L. Bryan, Andrew M. Bryce, and Jennifer Roberts, "The Effect of Mental and Physical Health Problems on Sickness Absence," *The European Journal of Health Economics* 22, no. 9 (December 2021): 1519–33, https://doi.org/10.1007/s10198-021-01379-w.

Non-Standard Employment around the World: Understanding Challenges, Shaping Prospects, Geneva: International Labour Office, 2016.

Mental Health Policy, Plans and Programmes: Updated Version, Rev. ed., Mental Health Policy and Service Guidance Package, 2,1, Geneva: World Health Organization, 2005.

59   Hunnicutt-Ferguson, Wyka, Peskin, Cukor, Olden, and Difede, "PTSD and Impairment in Disaster Workers."

60   For a more extensive review of the effects of stress on cognition in law enforcement, please read *Processing Under Pressure*, by Matthew Sharps:

      Matthew Joseph Sharps, *Processing under Pressure: Stress, Memory, and Decision-Making in Law Enforcement,* Third edition, Flushing, NY: Looseleaf Law Publications, Inc, 2022.

61   For information on making adaptive decisions rather than rigid responses under stressful situations, see the following references:

      Lydia Morris and Warren Mansell, "A Systematic Review of the Relationship between Rigidity/Flexibility and Transdiagnostic Cognitive and Behavioral Processes That Maintain Psychopathology," *Journal of Experimental Psychopathology* 9, no. 3 (July 1, 2018), https://doi.org/10.1177/2043808718779431.

      Heather A. Cameron and Timothy J. Schoenfeld, "Behavioral and Structural Adaptations to Stress," *Frontiers in Neuroendocrinology* 49 (April 2018): 106–13, https://doi.org/10.1016/j.yfrne.2018.02.002.

62   Myers and Wee, *Disaster Mental Health Services.*

63   Ronald Whalen, "In Defense of After-Action Reviews: The Art and Science of Small Unit Coping," *Military Review*, April 2010.

      Joseph A. Allen, Roni Reiter-Palmon, John Crowe, and Cliff Scott, "Debriefs: Teams Learning from Doing in Context," *The American Psychologist* 73, no. 4 (June 2018): 504–16. https://doi.org/10.1037/amp0000246.

64   "Norma Cruz Khan – 9/11 Pentagon Memorial."

65   LivingWorks, "ASIST Suicide Prevention Training Program," accessed May 16, 2019, https://www.livingworks.net/asist.

66 For information and resources for Master Resilience Training (MRT), please see the following resources:

"ARD: Master Resilience Training," accessed September 28, 2021, https://www.armyresilience.army.mil/ard/R2/Master-Resilience-Training.html.

Joaquin Selva, "Master Resilience Training (MRT) in the US Army: PowerPoint & Interview," *PositivePsychology.com*, November 28, 2017, https://positivepsychology.com/master-resilience-training-mrt/.

67 Joint Base Langley-Eustis, "'Freedom's Fortress' Deactivated after 188 Years of Service," accessed November 21, 2020, https://www.jble.af.mil/News/Article-Display/Article/258576/freedoms-fortress-deactivated-after-188-years-of-service/.

"Fort Monroe After Base Realignment and Closure (BRAC)," accessed November 21, 2020, http://www.virginiaplaces.org/military/fortmonroebrac.html.

68 "The Chesapeake Bay Impact Crater," accessed November 21, 2020, https://www.ndsu.edu/pubweb/~ashworth/webpages/g491/2002presentations/rhondaolson/webpage.htm#:~:text=Approximately%20 35%20million%20years%20ago,to%20be%201.3km%20deep.

69 These news articles tell the story of Cliff's Soldier's Medal award:
"Clifford Bauman – Recipient," accessed November 21, 2020, http://valor.militarytimes.com/hero/33606.

Virginia Guard Public Affairs, *Virginia Guardsman Awarded Soldier's Medal for Heroism*, July 23, 2010, photo, https://www.flickr.com/photos/vaguardpao/4822421552/.

70 *The Virginian-Pilot*, "Norfolk Marine, 75 Years | Anniversary Issue," accessed June 4, 2019, https://www.pilotonline.com/inside-business/special-reports/vp-ib-ai-norfolk-marine-0712-20210712-avow4cg4onafzbeve6c5fmn6r4-story.html.

71   "Soldier's Medal," n.d., https://military-history.fandom.com/wiki/ Soldier%27s_Medal.

72   CW4 Bauman's Soldier's Medal notes four sailors saved, which is a discrepancy from the actual number of three sailors. "Clifford Bauman – Recipient."

73   "Clifford Bauman – Recipient."

74   William Henderson, "Changes to the Security Clearance Mental Health Question," *ClearanceJobs*, July 6, 2013, https://news.clearancejobs.com/2013/07/06/changes-to-the-security-clearance-mental-health-question/.

75   Interview with Subject Matter Expert, September 10, 2019.

76   Ibid.

77   Joie D. Acosta, Amariah Becker, Jennifer L. Cerully, Michael P. Fisher, Laurie T. Martin, Raffaele Vardavas, Mary Ellen Slaughter, and Terry L. Schell, "Assessing the Department of Defense's Approach to Reducing Mental Health Stigma," *RAND Corporation*, January 18, 2016, https://www.rand.org/pubs/research_briefs/RB9881.html.

78   DVIDS, "Suicide Prevention PSA: CSA Raymond T. Odierno," accessed June 4, 2020, https://www.dvidshub.net/video/154428/ suicide-prevention-psa-csa-raymond-t-odierno.

79   DVIDS, "Retired Army General, Wife Share Story of Loss," accessed June 4, 2020, https://www.dvidshub.net/news/113713/retired-army-general-wife-share-story-loss.

80   DVIDS, "Suicide Prevention PSA: SMA Raymond Chandler," accessed June 4, 2020, https://www.dvidshub.net/video/154430/ suicide-prevention-psa-sma-raymond-chandler.

81 Interview with Behavioral Health Officer, December 20, 2019.

82 "Tragedy Assistance Program For Survivors (TAPS) Is Here For You!" accessed April 4, 2021, https://www.taps.org/.

83 SAVE, "SAVE: Suicide Prevention, Information, and Awareness," accessed November 29, 2020, https://save.org/.

84 "Survivors and Supporters Rally to Prevent Suicide on Capitol Hill | TAPS," accessed June 29, 2022, https://www.taps.org/articles/2019/prevent-suicide-rally.

85 "RUDAW," accessed March 20, 2022, https://www.rudaw.net/english.

86 "ABLE Channel," accessed August 29, 2022, https://the-ablechannel.com/.

87 "Veteran Trash Talk," accessed November 29, 2021, https://veterantrashtalk.com/.

88 Organizations searching for suicide prevention public speakers can contact Cliff through his website, *cliffordbauman.com*. He also receives requests through work and word of mouth, or when interested organizations find him from news stories or videos about him online. He does an average of twenty events a year. He talks with the person requesting his speaking and finds out what the organization is, what they need him to cover, and what they want to achieve. He tailors his speeches to the environment and situation, including the verbal and physical input he receives from the crowds. By being observant and adaptable, he can meet the audience's needs and give every group a personalized presentation.

Clifford Bauman, "The Mental Health Warrior," 2022, https://cliffordbauman.com.

ABOUT THE AUTHORS

CLIFFORD W. BAUMAN is a 34-year Army Veteran and an internationally known motivational speaker. As a survivor of an attempted suicide, he realizes the importance of getting counseling and having a strong support structure. Cliff hosts his own podcast, *The Mental Health Warrior*, on Veteran Trash Talk and Wreaths Across America Radio, and has published articles in *USA Today, Army, Navy, Marine and Air Force Times, GX Magazine, Newsliner, National Guard Association Magazine, Huffington Post,* and *RallyPoint.* Cliff believes that "Life Promotion" is the best suicide prevention.

WILLIAM D. KAMMERER is a forensic psychologist, Commissioned Army National Guard Officer and 21-year military veteran, and a former Army Suicide Prevention Program Manager of five years. He gained insight about suicide prevention from many special assignments, and utilized his background as a forensic psychologist to review investigation documents to determine the priorities Army leadership should focus on to stop suicide in its ranks. He met, traveled, and worked with CW4 (Retired) Clifford (Cliff) Bauman during a 6-month special assignment for the Army. While attending a "lived-experience" discussion panel at an American Association of Suicidology (AAS) conference, he realized the importance of Cliff's story and was inspired to bring it to a broader audience through a book. William is married with three children and is currently a research psychologist in the DC area. A Dostoyevsky enthusiast, he also enjoys classic cars, retro computers, and coaching his kids' sports teams.